WAR BABY

Rod Butler

ISBN: 9798732164145

Cover design by: Rod Butler
Library of Congress Control Number: 2018675309
Printed in the United States of America

Copyright thanks.
I would like to thank the Copyright owners of two pictures, notably the boy on the front cover, and the picture of the Anderson Shelter by CW Larson. These copyright owners cannot be found. Credit and thanks to the owners will be gladly added or the pictures removed if necessary.

I would like to thank my wife Lucy for her patience with me during the creation of this book. I would also like to thank my long term friends Chris Lafbury and Roger Rayner, and my Sister Jan Brady for their proof reading.

WAR BABY

A Story of a Life

by

Rod Butler

To the memory of my Mother and Father,

Lillian Ruby Edith Butler and Alfred Albert Butler

and

Dedicated to
My son and daughter Daren and Simone
and my wife Lucy

WAR BABY - PART 1

WAR BABY - PART 2

INTRODUCTION

T his book is not suitable for children and it should be treated as an 'X' certificate publication. Under 16's should definitely not have access to any of these pages, nor should anyone of a nervous disposition, or with a flagging or waning sense of humour. Anyone working for a law enforcement agency such as the Police should not be tempted to open this book. Anyone who is easily led or influenced should put this book down now and retire to bed with a nice warm mug of Horlicks. If you enjoy and are happy in the strange world of political correctness, this book is NOT for you. I guess that leaves about six of us in the world who can be described as 'qualified' to read on further. You are part of a very small but select and unique audience.

Everything in this book is true and some of it may shock the nervous, unhinge the hinged, or wake the departed. It is certainly a story never to be repeated!

I trust that we have now eliminated everyone who should not be here and that you are an adult, well balanced, sensible and intelligent person, an audience with your own point of view, your own opinion, not offended by other opinions, and uncontaminated by the peculiar political brain washing of the last two decades, with good looks and a vibrant sense of humour.

There is now just you and me.

Good!

We can start the journey.

Are you sitting comfortably?

Yes?

Then let's begin.

I have tried to write honestly and with the minimum of bias - if such a thing is possible, (I guess we are all biased toward our own interpretation of any one given thing). I have tried not to intentionally embarrass anyone, so please do not be embarrassed as this book is only written from my own point of view. Please accept my advance apologies however if you are in here and you are embarrassed; I will hold *you* responsible as *you* have given me cause to write something that may be embarrassing! Embarrassment is a strange emotion but it doesn't really serve any practical purpose. It's a bit like being naked in front of strangers, and that is just the feeling I experienced from writing many of these early pages; embarrassment, feeling naked, and so consequently the working title of this book was originally 'Nothing to Hide,' as I did feel as though I was undressing in front of a select audience of strangers and relatives who I had not seen for a very long time.

The writing of these pages took place between 2004 and 2020, at the instigation of my Sister Jan, who, at my 65th birthday party, had had a few drinks and suggested I write a book. Of course, being somewhat inebriated myself, I agreed.

The first and main part of this book is factual; an account of my early life and experiences. The second shorter part, is about my feelings and impressions about the world and life in general - a light hearted glance at the world in which we live. This is the difficult part, as I am aware that one's feelings and impressions can and do change. What I feel today I may feel differently about in a week, a month or a year's time. One's feelings and impressions change over time and so this second part of the book should possibly not be taken too literally. It is nevertheless important, as it could be viewed as a chronicle or even evidence of my eccentricity, (I am sure that there are some areas of my character that can be described as eccentric - to a degree, of course).

It has been particularly difficult, challenging and even at times upsetting to write this book. There is laughter and tears, pleasure and pain. Some of the memories make me sad and some make me laugh out loud. Such is life. I am sure that a psychologist could make something of the fact that I quite often drove myself forward into certain situations, against everyone's advice and against even my own common sense and better judgment. Maybe that is what life is all about, without the pain, upset and sorrow how are we to understand and enjoy the good times?

The reader may judge that my life was filled with pain, but this is certainly not the case and I am certainly not looking for any kind of sympathy; indeed, any pain has certainly been outweighed by the joy of actually being alive. I suspect that all people are the same - finding the balance between negative and positive or good and bad. I have always believed that good times and pleasure have to be paid for in some way - with pain as the currency, and so I consequently never envy very rich or very successful people, or the wealth and fame that surrounds and follows them.

I therefore hope that this little book brings you

some smiles, some frowns and maybe even some growls, clearing of the throat or flushing of the cheeks, enlightening you to the fact that you are not alone; we all feel the pain and the pleasure that life itself delivers to us at the most unlikely and sometimes at the most unsuitable of times.

As John Lennon once said; "Life is what happens while you're busy making plans."

And as Rod Butler says; "The important thing is not what you've got, it's what you DO with what you've got."

INNOCENCE

War is a time of noise, confusion, fear, shock and uncertainty, and for a small baby the effect of war is even more traumatic, being unable to speak or understand.

* * *

It was dark with just a candle flickering, throwing animal shapes onto the wall. I was scared and I could hear my Mother rapidly breathing. I was lifted and rolled quickly under the table with a whisper. There was wire fencing all around and I felt like an animal in a cage. Now the candle was blown out and I could see nothing. I felt the warmth of my Mother's body, her arms around me and her heart beating fast. Then the noise started; a terrible whining screeching noise like an enormous animal trapped, hurt and in pain. After a short while, the noise stopped and it was completely silent again. I wanted to get out of the cage. I wanted to go outside and look up at the sky. I wanted to be in the park and pushed along in my pram. My Mother held me firm as if I was part of her body. And then I heard the hum above from what seemed a long way away. The hum got louder and louder until I could hear nothing else – not even my Mother's breathing or heartbeat. My ears hurt with the noise coming from the sky, and then an even louder whistling, then crash and then more whistling and more crashes all around. The house shook and something fell off of the wall and smashed on the floor. More and more whistling, screeching and crashes all around. My head was full of noise. I wanted to scream out loud. I knew the smell of milk and the smell of the park but now I smelt something different, something nasty. It was a new smell that I didn't like and I didn't want. The windows shook and rattled and I felt dust on my face. I felt frightened and then suddenly it stopped – no more noise. I felt my Mother let out a long, long breath and then she whispered to me; "There there, we're alright now, it's over." I could once again hear the loud tick tock of the clock as if it was marching along - part of an imaginary army. My ears felt strange, as if everything was muffled; as if I was back in the womb, safe once again. I wanted to speak but didn't know the words. But then another strange noise started; still in complete darkness, but a smoother, lighter, happier kind of sound. "It's the all clear." My Mother rolled over and out of the cage underneath the table. She struck a match and lit a candle. The light from the candle made me feel warm and happy. She then stood up and took down the black curtain from the window. I tried to pull myself out from under the table. I was picked up and looked out of our window, our faces glowing gold in the candlelight. I could see lots of other happy candles now, flickering in windows along our road. The noise had gone, the candles were bright and happy, I could hear voices outside, but as my Mother lifted me up higher I could see smoke coming from a big gap in the road where a house used to be, eerily lit by the bright yellow smiling moon.

A Morrison Shelter used during the War when an air raid was in progress

Years later I learnt that we were hiding under a 'Morrison Shelter', something that could be used as a table during safe periods, and as an air raid shelter to protect us from German bombs during air raids. We were living at 42 Tretawn Gardens in Mill Hill, in North West London. My Mother and Father stayed in the London area during the war as my Father had the war job of a 'Fire Watcher' or spotter. When there were no bombs or air raids he worked for the Remington Typewriter Company in London. When the bombing and the fires became intense, he had to direct fire engines through the bomb damage to fires caused by the Luftwaffe bombers. His job also entailed covering incendiary bombs with sand to put out the flames and stop the fires spreading. There were also smaller fires which he had to extinguish with a hand pump and a water bucket. Small but dangerous butterfly bombs that the Luftwaffe dropped but that had not successfully exploded also had to be dealt with. These small, lethal bombs were dropped, sometimes hundreds at a time, and so if one was found it could be guar-

anteed that there would be many more close by. Some
bombs were even booby trapped, so that if picked up or
moved they would explode, killing whoever was nearby.
It is amazing that any fire spotters actually survived at
all with the danger of unexploded bombs that could explode or ignite at any minute. My Father survived the
war but died prematurely at the age of 50 just a few years
later. I consider that his premature death may have been
caused by the poisonous fumes inhaled from the chem-
icals contained in these bombs, which were dropped
onto London on an almost daily basis during 1940 and
1941 - the year of the Blitz.

My Mother and Father on their Wedding Day - 21st April 1930

There is, however, another possible side to the
story. Children were never involved in hearing news,

truth or the facts about important matters within family life. They were not, and probably should not, be interested in 'adult talk'. In the 40s and 50s children were 'seen and not heard' - and were generally not party to any of the more serious or important details of family life, and this is one of the reasons that this book exists; to tell the truth and the facts to anyone who may be remotely interested.

My Mother posing at the seaside before the War. This could be Babbacombe in Devon.

My Mother and Father happily on holiday before the War.

We were indeed told that our Father was a fire watcher (and I am sure that he was) but, during the war, the office in Holborn where he worked, was heavily bombed and subsequently razed to the ground. He was a typewriter mechanic; he worked for the Remington typewriter company and prior to the war travelled around the world for his work. I seriously wonder, with his skills in this field, if he was involved with the messages or even the code breaking that formed such an important part of our defence against Hitler. Details of his work during the war were not openly divulged to other members of the family, who in later years confessed that they knew little of his activities during that time, unlike many of the family uncles who related war stories at the drop of a hat. He was fit and so why was he working in Central London and living in West London when other young men of his age were taking part in the actual war? Naturally all intelligence or code breaking work was top secret and so it would not be surprising if details or information about such work was not forthcoming.

OK. I'll own up. I've been watching too many James Bond films! It's probably just my imagination and after all, the main World War 2 code breaking operation was based at Bletchley not in London.

When I was born, the blitz of London had finished and the air raids were just sporadic. The war, although still raging in various countries, seemed to be drawing to a conclusion. Terrible bomb damage was still caused by occasional air raids and by the V1 and the even larger V2 rockets that Hitler had developed, and consequently, full air raid precautions still had to be observed. Air raids were usually at night but the self propelled V1 and V2 rockets could arrive at any time during the day, with just the frightening whirring sound of the V1 or 'doodlebug' rocket announcing its deathly arrival, and then the silence of the engine stopping before the crash and explosion. V2 rockets were a totally different story; travelling faster than the speed of sound and arriving just a few minutes after being launched, there was no warning, no sound, just complete and utter destruction following the sound of the deafening sonic boom. The V1 and V2 rockets killed thousands during the last stages of the War, at a time when many thought that Hitler had been beaten and had lost the War.

My Mother wanted to keep us all together rather than split the family up, and so we stayed together as a family in Mill Hill, West London. Homes were very cheap to rent, as no one wanted to live in London during the war. During the actual bombing raids, we did have the opportunity to go into our neighbours 'Anderson Shelter' which was built like a corrugated iron hut, half submerged in the back garden, but my mother felt safer indoors hiding under the 'Morrison Shelter'; she said she didn't want to be "buried alive in someone's garden." It was just as well, as one poor family living not so far away, took a direct hit whilst in their own Anderson Shelter and the whole family was killed. There were aerodromes and railways near to Mill Hill, and I think that was the reason the bombers tried to target the area, often missing their targets and hitting homes instead. The German bomber pilots couldn't see what they were aiming at during the night, as all houses had 'blacked out' windows and all street lighting was turned off during air raids.

There was evidence of the country's efforts to defend itself years later when white rings could still be seen painted around trees that bordered roads, and kerb stones still remained, decorated with white paint. These white markings on trees and kerb stones helped pedestrians, cyclists and motorists keep to the road if they were caught out during an air raid or a blackout. Pill boxes (reinforced concrete defences) could be seen at the side of many country roads, although it is rare to see them nowadays. These defences were to be used as a last resort to defend against invading Germans, if and when they arrived. Inside homes it was also common to see pin holes around wooden window frames where black out cloth had been pinned. There were often hundreds of holes where the cloth had been put up and taken down over a long period of time. Bomb damage, especially in the City of London, was present for many years before eventually being repaired. Years after the war, many homes still had their collection of grotesque gas masks - one for each member of the family, including babies and children.

I was a 'war baby,' born in May 1944, towards the end of the second world war. My birth was celebrated - perhaps more than most, as my appearance in the world was actually quite a shock. My Mother and Father were married in April 1930 and longed for a baby, as many couples did before, during and after the war years, but they were told by the doctor that it was not to be. After failing to conceive during the first fourteen years of marriage, tests were performed and my Mother was told she would be unable to give birth, hence the surprise when, after all this time, I did actually arrive. It may be that one of the German bombs created such an explosion that my Fathers sperm got frightened and took refuge inside one of my Mother's eggs, giving me a chance to fertilise or become fertilised. Either way, the fourteen year delay in my Mother conceiving I regard as good, as I am actually fourteen years younger than I should be! My Mother's Brother, Clarence, was also unable to become a Father and so it may be that there was a genetic reason for the lack of births, although her other Brothers did become Fathers within their own marriages. When she did finally become a mother, I think there was a lot of joy and celebration, and probably bemused surprise as well!

Happier times before the War. My Mother and Father centre.

WHO AM I?

After the war had ended, was a naturally happier time. We could walk in the park, and being a baby, I could get pushed up and roll down Uphill Grove, Mill Hill in my pram. I loved going downhill with my Mother running, holding onto the pram. I used to laugh as she pulled faces at me whilst we were speeding down the hill. People would stop and talk to each other (my Mother was very good at this), as news and gossip were exchanged whilst on the way to or from the shops. I used to get very bored with these interruptions, as I could not talk and join in with the laughter and chatting. There were things that I wanted to say, but I just hadn't learned to speak properly - I just made funny noises. Everyone seemed to like my noises and efforts to talk, and they made noises back at me. I couldn't understand their noises though, and I thought "why don't you talk properly to me?" There were quite a few babies like myself in prams, it seemed as though all ladies wanted to have a baby; I suppose that was the effect of the war and the feeling that you might get blown up by a bomb during one of those terrible air raids. Surely the bombs wouldn't blow up Mothers and babies though, would they?

We visited other local families as well, and where there were other babies or small children, I could play with their toys and try to talk. When we visited baby Lawrence's house, I remember he had a red wooden fire engine that I thought was wonderful. We played with it and had loads of fun; it was so good that I wanted to keep it and take it home. I started to cry when it was time to go home; I knew I would really miss that fire engine. I was allowed to take the red ladder that went on the roof of the fire engine home with me, but then he started crying because I was taking his ladder away. I suppose you could understand it; a fire engine is not much use without a ladder.

I started to try to walk after I had mastered crawling pretty well. I could walk and take a few steps whilst holding onto nearby pieces of furniture. It felt so good, as I could see from higher now, instead of just looking down at the carpet or seeing peoples' shoes! Now I knew what adults must feel like when they walk anywhere and can see everything.

As mentioned earlier, before the war my Father was a typewriter mechanic travelling to far off places, representing the company that he worked for - The Remington Typewriter Company. After the war finally came to an end, he became a photographer for a company called Polyphoto based at Hendon. He was a studio photographer, taking portraits of families, couples and of course babies and children. Lots of men in uniform with their wives had their pictures taken, and I remember he was always very busy. Children were I think, his favourite subject to be photographed, as he was very good with children and always made them laugh. I remember very clearly being photographed by my Dad in the Polyphoto studio in West London when I was about one year old. The result was a large page of tiny prints containing dozens of slightly different pictures. From this sheet of small pictures, a favourite could be chosen which could be enlarged for the wall at home, or given as a present to a relative. For my photographs I was dressed up in clothes that I didn't like and made to sit on a cushion that I kept falling off of. I didn't want to smile or laugh for the pictures as I was fed up. My Dad was determined to make me laugh, so he gave me a little toy to play with, and then from above and behind the camera he made funny noises. It made me laugh, although I didn't want to. He did it again and again and dozens of pictures were taken. The pictures were taken with both of us happy in the end. I saw all of the pictures later on, and one that my Mum liked was enlarged and framed, and I remember it hanging on the wall at home.

Then exciting things started to happen. I discovered I could talk a bit but understand even better. I could tell what people were thinking just by the look on their faces. I could make people smile by just pulling a face or making noise. Then the news arrived; We were to have a new baby! I might get a sister or a brother but we didn't know which yet. I thought it was a bit silly to get a baby and not know whether it was going to be a boy or a girl. This was very frustrating for me and I kept asking "Am I going to have a Brother or a Sister?" I didn't mind which, but I just wanted to know. Boys didn't like you playing with their toys but most girls didn't mind, so probably at that point I would have preferred a Sister. Years later I was glad I got a sister who turned out to be the most wonderful sister anyone could have wanted, in spite of the fact that most of her toys were dolls.

Whilst the preparations for our new baby were being made I felt a bit abandoned, as if no one was interested in me any more. We hadn't run down the hill in the pram for ages and everyone had stopped looking at me and stopped pulling faces and making noises. I had also heard that we were moving home and were going to live in Bush Hill Park with my Father's Mother – my Grandmother, whom I had never met. I remember travelling by bus and train and reaching Bush Hill Park Railway Station. The station had exits on each side of the platform, and each exit lead to a different part of Bush Hill Park. We came out of the station from the wrong side, and we had to go into a sweet shop to ask where Millais Rd was. Bush Hill Park is split into two by the railway line that runs from Liverpool St to Enfield - split into good and bad, or posh and rough. The shopkeeper explained that we need to be on the other side of the railway line to get to Millais Rd. We were on the 'posh' side of Bush Hill Park and Millais Rd was on the 'rough' side. Eventually we found my Grandmother's house (my Fathers Mother), which was dark and cold inside. Everything looked very old, but my Grandmother seemed like a nice kind person. I sat and looked out of the tall French Windows. It was dark and different to the place at Mill Hill where we had been staying; it didn't seem quite as nice. My Grandmother was sitting down and wearing a white lace shawl around her shoulders and a very long black dress. I had never seen anyone dressed like that before, and never seen anyone so very old.

I can't remember actually moving in – it may be that our first visit <u>was</u> the time when we moved in. My Mother and Father had little in the way of belongings, as all of the furniture at Mill Hill belonged to the owners of the property. It was 1948, the war had finished and the owners of our home at Mill Hill wanted their home and their furniture back. I know that we were on the council house waiting list for many years and that my Mother hoped we could get into a council house. I also remember her telling me that there was a ten or twelve year waiting list for a council house, as so many homes had been destroyed during the war and there were not enough homes available for everyone.

We soon settled in and I slept in a small bed upstairs, just above my Nan's 'back room'. I couldn't get used to the bed or the room, and I remember often waking up facing the wrong way with my feet on the pillow where my head should have been and my head at the other end of the bed where my feet should have been. I think my Dad realised that the move was taking a bit of getting used to, because on Fridays when he came home from work, I was allowed to stay up late to see him.

Sometimes my Mother took me to the Cambridge Road (the A10) to wait for him to arrive at the bus stop. We seemed to be waiting for ages, my hungry eyes searching the brow of the hill over which the red bus from Turnpike Lane underground station would appear. The small red dot in the distance on the brow of the hill gradually enlarged until it slowly grew into the rest of the bus. The odd car came by, but quite often there would be no traffic until my Dad's bus appeared. I looked forwards to these Fridays and he often brought home a special treat of cream cakes or sweets. The cream slices were everyone's favourite. I was not really interested in cakes or sweets though, I really preferred the more unusual treats, and sometimes I would get a handful of different coloured bus tickets collected on his way home from Turnpike Lane underground station to Wood Grange bus stop on the Cambridge Rd. I loved these tickets and used to set them out on the floor in patterns. Sometimes I would imagine I was a bus conductor giving tickets out to all of the passengers, and one day my Dad gave me a very special gift - something that no one else had and something that I dreamed of owning. It is a bit difficult to explain, but in those days a bus conductor had to walk around while the bus was moving and take payments from the passengers on his bus. As he walked around, he put the payments into a large leather bag around his shoulder and issued the passenger a coloured ticket for the journey. This was the exciting bit; the different coloured tickets were held in a special ticket holder - a small hand held rack with springs to hold the tickets in place - different coloured tickets according to each passenger's destination. Passengers' tickets would then be validated with a hole that was punched through with a small silver machine that the conductor also carried around his neck.

My Dad gave me the best ever present I ever had; he had made a bus conductor's ticket rack complete with springs and used coloured bus tickets. I was so excited, so thrilled. My imagination ran wild as I played, with imagined bus journeys and tickets being issued to hundreds of imaginary passengers on exciting journeys.

The best treat ever was some small sheets of photographic or 'magic' paper. To me this paper really was magic, and I could make silhouette pictures by just holding the paper close to the light in the ceiling with any item held in front of the paper. We had gas lights at that time and so you had to be careful not to burn the paper or your fingers. The best picture that I made was a pair of scissors. I just laid the scissors onto the paper and held everything towards the light for around ten seconds. I took the scissors away from the paper and there it was – my magic picture of a pair of scissors. I made other magic pictures using a toothbrush, a tea strainer, and a fork. I loved doing this and can still feel the excitement even now years later as, held safely by my Father, I balanced on a chair reaching up towards the gas light filament with my magic paper, waiting for the picture to appear.

My Mum and Dad also used to make things; sweets! In the larder there would be a tray with lots of different coloured sweets on. Sometimes it would be sugared almonds and sometimes coconut ice or candy of some other description. I never got to eat many of these homemade sweets so I don't know who ate them all! That's the thing about being a child; there are lots of things that you don't know!

Suddenly one day my baby sister arrived. I didn't know where she came from but I was glad she had finally arrived. Now I had someone to play with and talk to. I must have been three or four at the time and I was getting inquisitive. I wanted to know where the baby came from. I wanted to know everything. I even wanted to know what that 'pink thing' was underneath my Nan's cat's tail. I used to speak to my Nan and wanted to know what her breasts were for! She explained to me that they made the milk for the baby, but that all of her milk had now dried up. I wanted to know why there was a picture on the wall with a little book of numbers underneath it. It was a nice little book, a miniature. She explained that it was a calendar and I didn't understand at all. Why do we need to know the number of the day? We know the next day is tomorrow and the day before is yesterday! It was difficult for me to understand but she tore the little book from the picture on the wall and gave it to me to take to bed. My Dad carried me upstairs in my pyjamas and I held the little book and the candle which lit our way. I was not allowed to hold candles that were alight but this candle was in a candle holder which had a small tray to catch the melted candle wax, and a special handle that kept your fingers away from the flame. The candle holder was green. I liked carrying the candle.

I had to be very careful with my sister, and was not allowed to play with her until she got a bit bigger. She always seemed as though she wanted to play though. She laughed a lot and didn't cry much. I could make her laugh quite easily and enjoyed seeing her laughing and gurgling. I knew what it was like to be a baby and knew that eventually she would be able to talk properly. I felt as though she had always been there and forgot what it was like before she arrived.

My Sister Jan and I, playing in Grovelands Park

I still liked rides on the pram. I was too big to be in the pram as it was now my sister's only means of transport, but I used to climb up and sit at the end, holding onto the handle so as not to fall off. My favourite ride was sitting on the pram and going through the park known as 'Bush Hill Park.' The path through the centre of the park was lined with chestnut trees. There were football pitches, tennis courts and lots of beautiful flower beds. It was these flower beds that always caught my attention. The colours, the reds, oranges, and yellows. At this time of the year there were beds of brilliantly coloured tulips. My Mum stopped the pram to admire the carpet of colour exclaiming "Look, aren't those flowers beautiful?" and in my first experience of giving (and taking) I said "Would you like some Mum?" Without waiting for an answer I slid down from the pram and ran from the path

27

over the grass to the flowerbeds. I knelt down and started carefully picking the tulips, ignoring my Mum's voice calling out for me to come back quickly. I picked a nice mixture of colours, as many as I could hold. I heard my Mum's voice calling me loudly again but carried on picking. Then, I heard a deep voice from above saying sternly "And what do you think you are doing young man?" I looked up at the enormous uniformed park keeper and realised I was doing something wrong just by looking at his face. "I'm getting some flowers for my Mum." My small voice was trembling. "Give them to me and don't let me catch you doing that again or I will take you down to the police station!" He took the flowers from me and I ran back to the pram with tears in my eyes. I quickly jumped on, and as my Mum pushed us through the park I thought I heard her silently giggling to herself. I expect the flowers ended up with the wife of the park keeper disguised as a thoughtful gift from her husband!

I don't know when or how my Grandmother passed away, but I do remember having to stay with some distant relatives who lived some way away. This may well have been the time of my Grandmother's death, a time when children were not necessary. I stayed with my Uncle Clarrie and Aunty Winnie in Nottingham and some other relatives who were not quite so far away. These relatives were quite nice, but more interesting than talking to them, was the fascination that I had for a ship in a bottle that was standing on their sideboard. I had never ever seen a ship in a bottle before and looking at it created stories in my mind about ships and seas. Naturally I wondered how the ship got into the bottle and thought about ways to get the ship out. They must have realised my fascination with this ornament and got it down for me to have a closer look at. They wanted me to go to bed but I wanted to stay up and play with the ship in a bottle. A deal was made. I would go to bed with the ship in a bottle. I played with it, feeding my imagination every day that I stayed with that kind family. When I eventually returned home my Grandmother was not there anymore. No one told me what had happened. I was sad.

My Father and Mother with my Father's Mother

I was growing fast and would soon be starting infant school. My sister was also growing, and she was more fun now that she could walk a bit, play 'hide and seek' and 'catch' with me. We had a nice garden and although quite small, there were some nice flowers and bushes growing there. Later in the summer, there were also gooseberries and loganberries to pick and eat. The summers were endless and we had good fun playing in the garden and even trying to grow plants and vegetables ourselves from seed.

I had my first year at Bush Hill Park Infant School. Going to school was a big shock and, at that point, I realised what calendars were for. Well, you didn't want to arrive at school on a Saturday or Sunday did you? I didn't like leaving my home or leaving my Mother to go to school. I could not understand that being at school was temporary and at some point I would be going home again. In my mind I always thought it was permanent imprisonment and this frightened me.

School introduced me to a whole new world of experiences, some good and some not so good. During one class we were played a recording of 'Sparkey's Magic Piano'. I loved that music and was transfixed by the sound of the voice sounding like a piano. It was a magical story and a magical sound. Once a week there was a 'Country Dancing' class which all boys and girls had to participate in. The girls loved it but the boys hated it and just wanted to escape from the class. My own mind was still on Sparkey.

The boys' toilet or urinal in the playground was a walled affair with no roof. The biggest and oldest boys could direct their wee over the wall and on to any poor child (preferably a girl) on the outside of the wall who happened to be playing there. Boys who could do this were looked up to and considered very clever or special. On one occasion whilst at home, I got into great trouble by threatening to 'wee over the wall' when I couldn't get my own way over something. I got into big trouble over that. What happened at school was not allowed at home.

School also gave me an introduction to punishment. I was reprimanded and told off for farting very loudly when the class was standing silently in single file, waiting to go into assembly. "Such a loud noise from such a small child" one of the teachers exclaimed. It was a great fart and the whole class erupted in laughter. That was my own very early first introduction to the world of entertainment. I enjoyed creating that laughter. Punishment could sometimes be harsh and again, whilst waiting in single file to enter the school after playtime, I accidentally dropped my 'cap-bomb.' The loud bang made the girls scream and I was marched off to Miss Stringer's office. Miss Stringer was the large and formidable headmistress of the infant school and, after a severe telling off, my cap-bomb was confiscated until the end of the week, when I had to return and ask for it back (properly, with an apology). I considered that Miss Stringer and indeed all girls were against boys because we had cap-bombs. I should explain that a cap-bomb is a small cylindrical bomb shaped lead weight, split into two pieces and tied together with string. A 'cap' (used in toy guns) could be inserted between the two flat sections of the bomb and, after being tied together with a slip knot, a 'bomb' was formed. The cap bomb could be dropped behind girls or thrown some distance to land near them with quite a loud bang, which always made the girls scream. The percussion of the two sections pressurised the cap inside causing the bang. If you really wanted to create a big bang, two caps could be used back to back instead of one. I loved cap bombs and eventually got my own one back from Miss Stringer, after I gave a full apology of course.

I always hated school. I hated the iron railings around the school playground, the shiny brown tiles in the corridors, the green and cream paint in all of the class rooms, the country dancing that boys had to do with the girls, and of course the smells. Classrooms had a smell, teachers had smells, toilets had smells, but of course the worst smell of all was school dinners. The pre-cooked ingredients for dinners arrived in large aluminium urns, much like the ones used by farms to transport milk. Mashed potato in one, greens in another, stew in another. The container which carried 'greens' - dark green soggy leaves which I am sure were not cabbage leaves at all but the discarded leaves of brussels sprouts and cauliflower, had a particularly pungent smell, one that I am sure could have been used for rodent or pest control. Even now, decades later, the sight of one of those aluminium urns in a totally innocent environment, brings back the memory of that awful smell. We all hated greens and I don't know why the school persisted in trying to get us to eat them, as most ended up on the floor, under a plate or disguised in some other way. The regular desert was prunes and custard. Try giving any child prunes, they won't be eaten. The smell alone is toxic and made most of the children eating school dinners feel sick. The various smells of school dinner ingredients became impregnated in the wooden building in the school playground - the place where we sat for those awful meals. As you approached the building the smell increased so that upon entering, you did not feel hungry at all, you held your nose and just wanted to escape! One day I did actually escape. I sneaked out of the playground, ran home, and lying, told my Mum that "the dinner ladies haven't arrived." The lie was transparent and I was punished accordingly - not for missing school dinner, but for lying.

There was never much money in our family. I got the feeling that other families were better off than us, but it didn't bother me at all; in fact all of the families in the area were probably just as poor. Our house in

Millais Road was rented and Mr. Tweedy came knocking on the door every Friday evening to collect the rent. I remember him being told on more than one occasion to come back next week for the rent. None of this bothered me until I pleaded for a new winter macintosh. I wanted one of those light khaki macs with the belt and the extra pockets, the same as a lot of the other school kids were wearing. It was explained to me that this was an 'extra expense' that we could ill afford. Eventually, and probably with great hardship, my parents presented me with my new mac. I wore it once before getting it ruined with white paint on my way home from school. Ron Taylor and I were playing 'football' with a half empty can of white paint - (Ron also appears later on in adult life), the can burst open and I was the one who got covered in paint. I felt awful and I was punished when I got home. The new coat hung on the wall smelling of turpentine and paint. It didn't get worn again and I didn't ask for any new items of clothing for many years. I was cold going to and from school, but I guess that was part of my punishment. Years later I had another accident with a can of paint; it was Guy Fawkes night and the bonfire – (everyone had a bonfire even if they had no fireworks) – was raging. An old can half full with paint was flaming brightly atop of the fire and I thought the can of flames would look good on the end of my fire prodding stick. The stick went into the can and I lifted it out of the fire and high into the sky. Flames and molten paint dropped out of the can and onto my wrist. My wrist was aflame and I was screaming with pain. After dousing with water and seeing the doctor, I was bandaged and left to feel sorry for myself. "Its your own fault for being so stupid." I always learnt from rather painful and unhappy experiences.

At home in the Winter, the fire had to be lighted with wood before the coal could catch alight. One of my small jobs was to make 'spills' which could be used instead of wood (which cost money). Spills were made from old newspapers. One page was rolled up and then twisted into a tight stick shape. The spills burnt very slowly and gradually the coal laid on top of them caught light and the fire got warmer. "Rodney, can you make some spills please?" was a common request from my Mother during the Winter months. Coal for the fire was delivered to the front door by the coal man. Sacks of coal were brought into the house and then the coal was dropped into the coal hole, which was actually the space underneath the stairs accessed by a door in the kitchen. Coal dust was always visible throughout the house as a result of these coal deliveries, and our coal fire, plus of course the trains, which were all powered by coal in those days. We lived just a few minutes away from Bush Hill Park railway station which meant that our curtains and paint work had to be regularly washed as a result of dust from the trains. I remember the joy on my Mother's face when the coal powered trains were replaced with electric trains and the curtains and paint work remained clean for weeks after being washed. She loved those electric trains.

As a result of the war ending things really changed. People became more grateful for even the most basic things in life; butter, eggs, milk, clothes and things that during the war were almost impossible to obtain. Ration Books were still needed in order to buy an egg, a loaf of bread, a packet of butter or an ounce of cheese, but people were happy that they could queue up and actually obtain small amounts of these day-to-day necessities, which during the war were classed as luxuries. The ration book would be inspected by the shop keeper to remove the token for essential goods, and confirm that nobody got more than their fair share of rations. It was a fair system, but I imagine there were fiddles and abuses going on behind the scenes. Rationing in Britain finished in 1954, nine years after the War had ended.

Clothes were much harder to come by as clothing materials were used during the War to supply British forces with uniforms and boots. I discovered a letter in my Mothers 'Deed Box' from her good friend Celia: The local news and gossip was mentioned, but at the end of the letter there was a paragraph offering her own son's pair of shoes to my Mother; "Clarke's brown lace ups, size 10 in good condition, cost 24/3, but you can have them for half price as he has grown out of them." I imagine my Mother jumped at the chance of getting me a virtually new pair of shoes at half price. (24/3 is around £1.20 in today's decimal money, so my new shoes were bought for around 60p).

Ten years after the end of the war however, rationing had just ended, but the scars were still evident in London's West End. On a children's Church trip to the London Palladium to see Norman Wisdom, there was still bomb damage in many areas, albeit decorated with wild plants and various weeds growing from what was left of the buildings and offices that were razed to the ground during the Blitz.

Money was always scarce, there was however money to be made by us youngsters. Beer and lemonade bottles, in fact most soft drink bottles, were made with thick strong glass and these bottles carried a small deposit paid by the customer when the drink was purchased and returned to the customer when the empty bottles were taken back to the off-licence. The deposit, usually just one or two pennies, was often ignored by the more well off and so it was just a matter of searching for these bottles near dustbins or rubbish sites and collecting them up. If ten or fifteen bottles could be collected, there was a nice amount of money that could be claimed when the bottles were returned to the off-licence. Certain makes of drinks could only be returned to certain off-licences which were contracted to sell selected makes of beer or soft drinks, and so there was an amount of skill involved in choosing the correct bottles to be returned to the various off-licences in the area. The staff of an off-licence where the wrong bottles were returned would always eye you suspiciously stating "Its not one of ours," if you took the wrong bottles back to claim the deposit. We sometimes cheekily collected beer bottles from the back yard of some pubs and took them around to the off-licence at the front of the building to claim the deposit back! The cheek of it! From these same off-licences I remember bottles of Creme de Menthe and Cherry Brandy being bought at Christmas time years later.

As youngsters we had to use our imagination to have fun or get a few pennies to buy sweets with. We had fun with our 'jiggers', a precursor of todays skateboard, but something that was made and not purchased in a shop. Four old pram wheels and some wood would need to be found - usually in a dump or rubbish tip of some kind. Our favourite rubbish dump for finding this kind of thing was 'the dell', an old piece of scrap land at the junction of Lincoln Rd and the Great Cambridge Road in

Bush Hill Park. The large BMW car showroom now sits where the dell used to be, and it was here that we would find the wood, wheels, bolts and string to make our jiggers. A plank of wood would be used as the main body with a pair of wheels attached to the front and the back of the plank with smaller pieces of wood. The front pair of wheels were steerable, as a revolving bolt would be used to secure the wheels, together with a piece of string that could be used to pull the wheels to the left or the right. You had to kneel on the central plank with one foot off of the floor, and push the jigger along with the other foot on the pavement. One shoe would always become worn out with toes sticking through because of the pushing done with that foot. There was a certain kind of status attached to these jiggers and some lads achieved great respectability by having an upholstered pad on the plank for their knee to rest on, or an extra large pair of pram wheels fixed to the rear of the machine. The jigger became part of you and described your personality; some jiggers fell to bits, some were luxurious, some were purely functional, some were built for speed and could not be beaten, some of them just looked great.

I always found school a bit of an ordeal and never really came to terms with the disciplined way of education. I preferred the more creative side of lessons such as nature study where I could draw pictures of flowers or birds. I had now moved up to junior school but still felt lonely and isolated. Each student had to read aloud from a book in class and I remember the great difficulty that I had pronouncing the word 'the.' The other children in the class would laugh at my efforts in trying to say this, most simple of words. I found 'the' very difficult. 'T – e' 'T – he' - and stammered trying to pronounce it.

* * *

There was a great geography teacher who taught us about all the countries of the world. During our time out of school we had to find labels from cans of food, vegetables or fruit boxes and even the small sticky labels found on apples, oranges and bananas. These labels often had the country of origin printed on them, and linked to a large wall map of the world with coloured pieces of string, we learnt where various countries were and what foods these countries produced. Oranges and dates from Israel, lemons from Italy, apples from France. That's how I liked to learn - by discovery. Even now, I still look at the labels on fruit or on the fruit boxes themselves, to see just where the produce was grown. I forget his name but he was a good teacher and he got us all thinking about geography and food production. A good teacher remains in your mind for life, but it seems to me now that the teacher's *enthusiasm* is the single most important thing to ignite a childs mind.

ALONE

'Look after your little Sister' – My Dad

My father had become very ill. He always used to use bicarbonate of soda. It was always in the larder, and was used for some considerable time to treat his 'indigestion'. There were coloured capsules in the cupboard - maroon, orange, yellow. He became more and more ill and had to go to hospital. The doctor's continual insistence that he had indigestion was the wrong prognosis; he had cancer which, by the time he was admitted to hospital, had gone through his whole body. The bus ride to Chase Farm hospital in Enfield was quite exciting but I was always disappointed when we got there as I was not allowed in to see my father. I had to stay put outside on a seat by the wall of the hospital and just underneath the windows of the wards for cancer treatment. My father made me happy one day when he looked out of the open window of the Capetown Ward above and called down to me. We both waved to each other but, of course, being so young, I didn't realise at that time how ill he was. I think he knew he was dying. He did return home once or twice after being in hospital and then I could see that he was very ill. He was often sick with a bowl on his lap, his false teeth falling into the bowl of sick. I got used to these kind of events and, subconsciously, told myself that it was normal – in order to cope with it I suppose. The stress came out in other ways though. I peed myself at my desk in school as I didn't have the confidence to put my hand up and ask to be excused. I still wore shorts and my legs, socks and shoes were soaked. I became desperately shy and insecure. I didn't want to go out or see any visitors. My father was moved from hospital to a hospice. The Hospice was organised by nuns who looked after terminally ill patients. It was some way away, and my sister and I, who were not allowed to visit him, were left with Mrs. Gabriel our next door neighbour, who would look after us until our Mum returned from her visits to the Hospice. Although I never saw him in the Hospice my Dad sent me a little note from Chase Farm Hospital, written very neatly in pencil telling me to look after baby Janice and my Mum. It was the very last communication that I had from my Father, and is now certainly my most valued possession. One of my other possessions is an old photograph album that belonged to my Father. Being a keen photographer he took many photos in London's West End, but the album contains pictures of his travels in distant lands, small pictures but showing great detail. He was well travelled. I would have enjoyed asking him about these countries and his travels had I had the chance.

One day Mrs. Gabriel came into our house to look after us instead of us going into her house. Our Mum came home later and told us that "Daddy has gone to be with the angels." I asked "Does that mean I can't see him?" and my mum replied with tears in her eyes "Not for a very long time." The funeral took place in St Marks

Church, Bush Hill Park and the burial was at Edmonton cemetery in Church St. I was not allowed to go to the funeral or the burial but I do remember looking after my Sister in the small park at the junction of the Cambridge Rd and Church St. I didn't know why we were there in this strange little park but just accepted it, not knowing that my Dad was being buried just a few short yards away. We didn't have a Dad anymore, but again, I took it in my stride, not realising that I was burying deep these important emotions. This, and the events of the next few years created in me a child who was quiet, withdrawn, introverted and painfully shy.

A break in Scotland was arranged and we travelled by train (the 'Flying Scotsman' I believe), up to relatives who lived in Newton Mearns near Glasgow. Uncle Sammy and Auntie Minnie were not really related to us, but for some strange reason were always known to us as Uncle and Auntie, and we got the chance to go up and stay with them for a few weeks. I think the trip was meant as a relief for my Mother who had seen her husband succumbing to his illness over a long period of time. It was an adventure and I played with the two sons, Michael and Martin who were both older than me. I think they had been told to play with me and look after me but I didn't feel the friendship was genuine. It was a Jewish family and I remember the Friday evening meals, very formal and traditionally Jewish. There were things that you had to eat like the paste made from the inside of chickens, spread on very thin toast. I didn't like it but had to eat it so as not to appear ungrateful or rude. I had never seen a telephone in anyone's house before and I was fascinated by listening to people talking on the phone. I remembered the number; Newton Mearns 2629, which was always the first words spoken when the phone was answered; "Hello, Newton Mearns 2629." Nevertheless, I was glad to get back home to familiar surroundings and familiar food, in spite of the fact that we did not have a telephone, a car or a big house like the family in Scotland had. Times were difficult and our mother had to go and claim social security benefit. She hated doing this and I remember once going to the 'Institute' in St. Marks Road with her to claim her benefit. (The broken down building then known as 'The Institute' is now a luxury block of flats). She came out of the office with a few shillings in her hand saying "I hate their money," but she had to take it as things were quite bad. There was a stigma to getting social security benefit in those days and she tried to make her visits to the institute as unnoticeable as possible. She always used to say to me "Money is your best friend." I only understood what she meant later when I learnt that she had watched her own mother squander away the family fortune on alcohol and binges at a local pub in Bedford – her home town. Her own faith in God was unshakable and it was not unusual to hear the words "God will take care of things" or "God will take care of us."

In our own way we became a small but close family group. We all seemed to support one another, and I was encouraged to look after and take care of my little sister. I was told to make sure that she gets to and from school safely, with the threat of, "The Bogey Man will get you if you don't come straight home after school." I never did have sight of the Bogey Man and now my imagination recoils at the thought of what he must look like. A giant slimy bogey with arms legs and head? Scary stuff.

My Mother took on homework which my sister

and I helped with. These were menial jobs that could be done outside of the factory and in poor people's homes. I remember us all sitting around the table during the evenings making paint brushes. These were the small brushes that artists use and not large commercial brushes for painting houses. For this work, the items were delivered to us and then the finished brushes collected the following week. We used to get hair - usually squirrel hair, string, boxes of the metal ferrules for the brushes, and brass 'cannons' that held the hair in the shape that was required for the brush. The hair had to be placed into the small brass 'cannon' so that the shape of the brush tip became pointed. A small piece of string was then tied tightly around the protruding part of the brush, which was then taken out of the cannon and pushed tip first through the metal brush holder - the piece that the artist holds when painting. The wooden handle was added by someone else at a later stage. I think we earned about one penny for each brush that was made and probably made no more than a few shillings each week. Times must have been very difficult for us, but these events and memories instilled in me a sense of independence – the importance of not having to depend on anyone else for financial security. Thus, I have always worked, made money and been financially secure, except for a short and unfortunate period of time when I myself had to claim social security benefit.

Christmas time meant my Sister and I making Christmas decorations. These 'Paper chains' were made during a period of several hours by gluing small strips of coloured paper together into a 'chain' which could then be pinned to the ceiling, one end near the light fitting and the other end pinned near to the wall. Repeated several times, the ceiling would be covered in brightly coloured paper chains ready for Father Christmas. This was always an exciting time because you knew Christmas was not far away. The excitement would build until at bedtime on Christmas eve, a long sock would be tied to the end of the bed. Even if you did your best to stay awake, you would eventually drift off to sleep and miss the visit of Father Christmas. My earliest memory of discovering my full sock on Christmas morning is still so very clear; the sock would be full - nuts, a couple of apples, an orange and then the real present from Father Christmas - something wrapped in Christmas paper. A mouth organ! I think I must have heard and enjoyed some harmonica music (maybe Larry Adler) and this was my Christmas present. I loved it, although I don't think I ever got the hang of playing it properly. It may be that the anticipation was better than the reality. We looked forward to things, particularly Christmas, for months before. The excitement built and grew during this time and I wonder if that was the part that was most enjoyable – the anticipation.

I was 9. It was 1953. The King had died and Queen Elizabeth was crowned queen of England. The war was long gone and there was a mood of optimism. Schools made a great point of using the coronation of the Queen as part of our lessons with pictures, stories and discussions about the event. We were all taken to a silk worm farm where we learnt how silk was made from the cocoons of silkworm moths, and we were shown how the silk was produced and coloured to actually make some of the Queen's regalia for the coronation. We learnt that the food for silkworms is Mulberry leaves, they love it and don't produce the silk without plenty of mulberry leaves. We unraveled silk worm cocoons and saw just how very fine the silk was. We were all amazed that the Queens Coronation clothes had been made in this way.

Everyone seemed happy and more and more people were filling up St Marks Church. The whole local community revolved around the church; I was in the cubs, my sister was in the brownies. I was in the choir and my mother was in the mother's union, as were most of the ladies living down our road. I loved the music of the church. I was never one of the best singers in the choir but the music inspired me. The melodies, the repetition, the building up of the melody; I still love Church and choral music, I find it most uplifting. It's all there in the hymns; the joy, the pleasure, the pain, the hope and the thanks.

There were still remnants of the war; ration books and coupons were now redundant but were still of use to children like us who wanted to play as shop keepers. The odd bullets and cartridge cases turned up at school and these were closely analysed by the older boys who could estimate the year of manufacture and the gun used to fire the bullet. A fearful cry went up from the teachers and the children one day when a lad came into school with a hand grenade. The charge of the weapon had been removed but it still looked pretty frightening with its lever handle, pin and tiled shrapnel surface. War, bombs, guns and bullets all seemed very exciting to me. I have always been fascinated by war, the way men can kill each other with bombs, guns and machines.

After school there were often visits to the local 'tuck shop'. A tuck shop is basically a sweet shop which caters for children and the small amounts of money they have to spend. 'Moodys' (long since gone), was in Main Avenue opposite the entrance to Bush Hill Park and there was often a large group of young children in the shop, or if they had no money, playing around outside. Moodys was a shop where a child could go shopping with one penny or even a half penny, and satisfy the urge to shop. One penny (1d) lollies were great value as they lasted a long time and tasted pretty good too. The proprietor of the shop - an aged Mr Moody - invented the one penny lolly himself and if he had taken out a patent on it he would have ended up quite a rich man. In his freezer he kept racks of metal lolly moulds. These were individually filled with fruity water plus lolly sticks and when frozen, supplied most of the children in the area with wonderful value for money in the ever popular one penny lolly. There were of course more extravagant purchases to be made; Flying Saucers, Black Jacks, Shrimps, Cough Candy, frozen Jubbly and Sherbet Dabs, but these were for special occasions when one had more than just one penny to spend.

Fun outside of school would be either marbles or cigarette cards which could easily be carried in a trouser pocket on the way to or from school. Marbles or cigarette cards could be collected and exchanged with others to build up a set, or they could be played, flicked or pushed, to win cards or marbles from other boys.

There were nice walks to be had in the Bush Hill Park area and we would often wander into the 'posher' parts of the area - Village Rd, Abbey Rd or Wellington Rd, my Sister being pushed along in the pram by my Mother with me trotting along behind. One day, whilst taking a stroll along Village Rd, my Mother stopped and admired the most beautiful little bungalow. Coloured glass decorated the arched front door, small statues of elves looked almost too real to be standing so still in the garden. There were flowers and small trees, hanging baskets overflowing with brightly coloured flowers and the sweet sleepy smell of lavender that bordered the front garden. There was a large 'FOR SALE' sign erected in the front garden and that attracted my Mothers attention. "Oooooh. Isn't it nice - I wonder how much it is." "Why don't we ask?" came my childlike response, and with that I was in the front garden and stretching up to knock at the front door. When the lady of the house answered the door I politely asked "How much is your house please?" She left the doorstep and went inside for a moment returning to say that the house would be around five or six thousand pounds. I said thank you, the front door was closed with a smile and I gave the news to my embarrassed Mother. She liked nice things so much but never really had any. I just wanted to please her and in my childlike way, thought that she could buy this very beautiful home. Of cause I got told off - with a smile. I always wanted to please her.

I was always very interested in plants, flowers and birds and during a visit to my Uncle Clarrie and Aunty Winnie's home in Bristol, this interest was secured permanently as part my character. The main thing I remember from this Summer Holiday with our Uncle and Auntie, was the garden. It was packed with unusual and exotic plants and vegetables. I had never seen marrows, artichokes and aubergines growing, and I was fascinated by the size of these plants and the size of the food that they produced. The large artichoke heads were one day quickly chopped off and taken in for dinner. They were boiled and we were taught how to scrape the fleshy part of the flowering head off between our teeth. It was the strangest kind of meal I had ever had - like eating a giant thistle. Cucumbers, tomatoes and lettuce were picked and used for salads and as well as fruiting trees and vegetables there was a greenhouse. The greenhouse was my Uncle's hobby, his pride and joy, and it was packed from floor to ceiling with Orchids, hanging from the roof and closely spaced on tiers of shelving. He imported the orchid tubers from various countries and grew them on to bloom in his heated greenhouse. These orchids were the original species, not the hybrid varieties that can be purchased for a few pounds in most shops and supermarkets today. The Latin names were detailed on labels planted in each pot, and he explained to me how rare some of these plants were and how he was looking forward to some of the blooms being produced. He explained the countries from where the tubers originated and the specific requirements of heat, nutrients and soil. He was a clever horticulturist and seemed to instinctively understand the needs of all of the plants in his garden and greenhouse. I enjoyed this visit and especially the fruit and vegetables that I saw growing in such abundance.

'Uncle Sonny' was a regular visitor to our house since our Dad had died and he especially liked looking after us children while our mother was out shopping or going about her chores. She was working hard to keep the family together. Social security had recognised the fact that she could not manage to support two children, and so there was talk that my sister and I might become individually fostered. My mum wanted to keep us both together and so worked daily, cleaning and scrubbing other people's houses. She would do two or sometimes three houses a day to earn money, just enough to stop Janice and I being taken away into foster homes. Mum was grateful for all the support from Uncle Sonny who used to be able to darn socks, mend shoes and repair clothing that had become worn or torn. He was a childhood friend of our own father while the pair were growing up in South Tottenham, and had spoken to our father during his final days saying that he would help look after 'Ruby and the children'. What a terrible betrayal was to take place.

Family holidays were taken at Shoeburyness, not far from Southend, in a caravan that was owned by 'Uncle Sonny' and one of his friends. There was no car and so these holidays included lots of walking as well as games played with other families staying on the caravan site. These games usually ended up with Uncle Sonny rolling around on the ground with myself and other young boys who were staying nearby. Being so shy and introverted I didn't like these close associations with boys that I hardly knew. My protests and upset were ignored and he continued with his rough and tumble games with other boys whenever he had the opportunity.

As well as doing small household jobs, he brought home stockings for mum from the factory where he worked which produced nylon stockings – 'Klingers' in Edmonton. He actually just lived round the corner to us in Leighton Road with his own mother and father, his sister and her husband. We saw more and more of him and he often took care of us going to bed. I didn't ever feel 'comfortable' near him; he asked questions such as "do you play with yourself" or "does your willie get big?" I knew something was wrong but couldn't understand what. He would take me to bed and then get in bed with me. He sometimes liked to wash and dry each of us with a towel beside the fire. Sometimes, when alone, he would play with my private parts and I didn't like it. I felt strange and I didn't want him to touch me. In bed and after my bedtime story, he would get his erect penis out. It looked like an enormous ugly thing, like a monster or a deformed balloon. He tried to get me to touch it and to hold it; I couldn't, it just looked so horrible. I didn't like looking at it, talking about it or touching it, it was horrific and frightening. He would masturbate and try to do the same thing to me. He once wore a condom and explained how good it was to reach a 'climax.' I felt I knew these things were wrong. I didn't know what to do. I just wanted to scream, to scream out loud, but I couldn't. Later on at school my head screamed. It was as if someone was inside my head screaming, but I was too scared to tell anyone about the person screaming inside my head. Unbeknown to me at that time, he did the same things with my little sister, who later on in life confided that she was always glad when he did his 'late shift' at work; working from 2.00pm to 10.00pm meant that we were asleep when he got home, and he could not put us to bed! He also used to say that he wanted me to stay as I was – a child, and never grow up. I could not understand and suggested in my childlike way that he put me in a small box so that I couldn't grow anymore. After that he used to say he was going to stop me from growing up. He did lots of things that were horrible when he was in bed with me or when he was drying me after being washed, and of course I know now that he was a pervert, or, as we more accurately say, a paedophile.

I feel nothing but contempt for these kind of people who prey on young children. I want to shout and tell them how they are scarring that child's life forever by feeding their own momentary sexually perverted desires. Dark feelings pervade my inner self when I think of how two boys, my Father and my step father - childhood friends, could grow up and play together, and then one of them could betray the other in such a ruthless and cruel way in later life. What on earth is it that drives a person to fuel such selfish acts of pleasure at the expense of a child's innocence? Being intimate with a small child in this way must reinforce their own adulthood, their own power, or their own importance.

Who could I tell? What would I say? Who would believe me? I just wanted him to go away and leave me alone. No other child or adult had ever spoken about these things and so it was actually difficult to comprehend what was going on, and of course being so young it was difficult to find the words to describe these events, even if I had the chance. There was no one there to look after me, no one to help me, no one who could understand, and my Mother was working most of the time. I was of course too young to know about or understand sexual feelings. I felt paralysed to talk to my Mother or anyone about what was going on.

Retribution came later on though - not from me, but from God.

Still lonely and insecure, I graduated from the Cubs to the Scouts. The regulation clothing had to be worn; shorts, long socks, shirt, scarf and of course a toggle which held the scarf in position. There were weekly meetings in St Marks Church Hall on the corner of Millais Rd, together with camping weeks away during holiday times. 'British Bulldog' was the game regularly played at our weekly Scout meetings, where teams had to run from one side of the hall to the other without being caught by the opposing team - the Bulldogs. Sing songs, camp fires and semi military boys games would be played whilst we were on camping trips, and it was not long before my step father acquired a Scouts uniform complete with shorts, and became part of the regular Scouts entourage. We all slept in tents, which we had to erect and midnight feasts would ensue, with bottles of fizzy drinks, sweets and biscuits. The adult leaders slept in a larger tent together. Of course my step father had only joined for one reason; to get close to young boys with view to 'grooming' them. It was obvious from the way he chased the boys around and enjoyed taking part in the boys games so enthusiastically. At least this took the pressure away from me; while lots of other boys were around, he left me alone.

Looking back now, there was a point when, if the Police had been more inquisitive, all of this could have dramatically changed. He would often go by bike to the park or to a lake - fishing. On one occasion, I was with him at the end of the Enfield Town Park by the New River. I didn't want to be with him and so I made my way to the opposite side of the river. He was alone and had his bike with him and as I watched, I saw two policemen approach him and start talking to him. I crouched down low out of sight behind some bushes. The talking went on for quite a long time and I continued silently watching as he was led away by the two policemen. I made my way home and explained to my Mother that he had been taken away by the Police. He didn't return until late that night, and in my effort to make him squirm, I sneeringly asked why he was taken away by the Police. "They thought I had stolen the bike" came the measured reply. My Sister and I considered that he had probably been watched at other times grooming young boys in the area. We never found out the actual truth of what did happen or why the Police took him away that day, but I am sure that if they had bothered to dig deeper and find the evidence, he would have been arrested and charged accordingly.

All of these things are now essentially said and spoken about. Many more other men and women in their middle ages are now speaking out about these terrible experiences that happened to them during their childhood, at home, in care, at school or even within the church. Half a century ago things like paedophilia were not spoken of. People either didn't believe things like this happened or didn't know what to do or say. They didn't want to deal with it, as problems would be caused for everyone in either the church, the school or the family if the actual truth came to light. It was actually too embarrassing to even talk about, so nothing was said. It was simply easier to bury your head in the sand and protect the guilty rather than appease, try to understand, or help the victim.

Of course I feel anger; anger at being used as a piece of pornography in some perverted dark imagination of the mind. Those in authority, be it in the home or other institution, have a duty to look after children in their care and to give them positive role models to follow. Paedophiles destroy that ideal, and plant a dark seed in the child's mind that can only grow and become a negative influence in later life. These experiences never go away; they are there for good and the child bears the scars of these memories and evil experiences forever. When children become adults, there is time enough for them to deal with the problems of relationships, sex and their own sexuality, and time enough for them to make decisions about sex and how it fits into their own private lives.

I have had to make an effort to not let these

events define my life. I have, since adulthood, made a point of talking about these experiences, so that I have control over how I am affected by them. Many have not, and experiences of perversion have defined who they are and what they do with their lives. I am amazed at how so many families and individuals have been affected by paedophiles - many are able to talk about these past experiences, but there are just as many who still say nothing and secretly carry the weight of their heavy burden around forever. Even now, I receive looks of incredulity when I tell this story. Even now, people find it difficult to believe or accept it as the truth.

Our poor angst ridden country stumbling along under the weight of political correctness and the fashionable 'human rights' brigade, seems to care more about controlling and restricting everyone's inbuilt prejudices, than about the actual real victims of crime and of course the victims of paedophillia.

The years went by and our Mum married Uncle Sonny. This did not please my sister or I, but being very young we had little influence in the proceedings. He was a chain smoker and stank. I didn't like him near me. I didn't like his voice or his face or the way he slurped his soup. Our mum didn't seem to notice our discomfort and was pleased when the 'New World' gas cooker arrived. The zinc bath hanging by a hook on the rear wall of the house was replaced by an indoor bath fitted upstairs. A new tiled fire place was put in, in place of the old black 'range', and a 'lean to' was added on to the back of the house. Electric lighting was installed instead of the ancient gas lighting. We couldn't believe how simple it was to get light into the rooms; just a flick of the switch on, and then off, instead of lighting the gas lamp hanging from the ceiling and waiting for the filament to glow and give out some light. The electric lights were switched on and off by my Sister and I as a kind of entertainment which annoyed my Mother who was usually preparing dinner. The hedge in the front garden was taken out letting more light into the front room, and we built a new front garden wall with a new front gate. I helped to mix the cement and put the bricks in place. Today, more than 70 years later, the wall and the gate are still standing at 7 Millais Rd.

At the time, I think my mum was very pleased with these improvements after she had endured such difficult times, but years later she confided; "I only remarried to keep you and Jan together, I didn't want you split up and have you both sent to separate foster homes." Whilst on her own, she had gone out to clean houses and had let two of the upstairs rooms to a lodger to help pay the rent and household bills. However, now we had a cooker, a bath and a new fireplace plus a stepfather who kept telling me he didn't want me to 'grow up.' He wanted to keep me as a child and to do this, he kept me in shorts when all other boys of my age were wearing long trousers. We stayed together as brother and sister but we both paid the price.

* * *

There was often a kind of political tension in the family apart from all of the other strange 'chemistry' between us all. My stepfather was a staunch Labour left winger and my Mother was always a Conservative. The differences came out in strange everyday ways, particularly with the reading of the daily newspaper. My stepfather always read the Daily Mirror – the 'Labour' paper. My Mother would not read this and called it cheap and lower class. She would only read the Daily Express – the 'Conservative' newspaper, which carried news that she understood and believed in. There were always political comments and innuendo in the household. The strange thing is that my Mother was more 'working class' than the average working class; cleaning seven pairs of her brothers shoes when she was a child, (she was the only daughter with seven brothers) and working in the dairy when she was still at school. The only work she ever did was housework or cleaning for other well off families. I don't know where my Mother got her conservative views from, but they have distilled in me and I am certainly more 'right' than 'left' when it comes to politics. I have always worked and not sponged from the 'state' – never been a 'freeloader' like so many who just want to get as much as they can for nothing, not putting anything back into society. One's politics must be genetic, or something that is picked up subconsciously from parents as comments fly back and forth. In any case, as a child, I seemed to understand that being a Conservative or a 'right winger' meant that you were hard working. Being Labour or left wing meant that you moaned a lot and stank of stale tobacco smoke.

It was 1954, I was 10 and jeans had arrived; Levis with great copper studs and stitching on the outside. On my way home from school one day, I noticed that the hardware store on the corner of our road (previously a pawn broker) had Levi jeans in stock. Some boys in my school wore them at school and were considered 'tough' or 'hard'. I saw the jeans as the opportunity to 'grow up' and become 'adult' and, apart from the fashion benefits, wearing a pair of Levi jeans must make you feel fantastic! After days of trying to get my stepfather to come to the shop to have a look, with a view to seeing a birthday present for my forthcoming birthday, he finally agreed. I was over the moon. We were going to actually see a brand new pair of jeans which will shortly be mine. I was too shy to ask the shopkeeper, but shortly the pair of jeans my size were laid out on the counter. They smelt new and tough and I ran my hands over the denim fabric and the shiny copper studs. What style! What design! So tough and strong they had to be held together with metal rivets! I had to have them. My excitement was uncontrollable. But, from the dizzy heights of excitement I was plunged to the depths of despair. My stepfather's only words were, "Maybe next year," as he turned me round and led me out of the shop. Such a simple thing would have made me so happy and maybe even more confident. It was not to be. Another year in flipping shorts and I was soon to move up to secondary school. I was still kept in shorts during my first year at secondary school and saw all of the other school kids my age happy and wearing long trousers.

Initiation was always part of school life and of course it was no different at Bush Hill Park Secondary School. New first year boys were put into 'The Pot' which was the large front school gate levered back, forming a triangular trap with the two adjacent corner walls. From there the older kids would climb up onto the gate and spit all over us new boys who were trapped in the pot. Dozens of older boys would spit or 'gob', and the new kids were covered in phlegm and anything else that could be coughed up by the older boys.

At 9.00am, we had to sit cross legged on the

school hall floor for assembly after firstly having a hand and shoe inspection. Hands, nails and shoes had to be clean, and there were punishments for those not conforming with these regulations of cleanliness. Being new, the only boy in shorts, and sitting in the front row for assembly, I was an obvious target of ridicule from the girls who filed into assembly from a different entrance to the boys. I hated this and wanted to cry. I was 10 and just wanted to creep away and be on my own or at least get a pair of long trousers.

The events of these early years had a dramatic effect on me. I was pathologically shy and blushed bright red if anyone looked at me. If anyone arrived at our house I had to run away somewhere and escape. I found it hard to talk to anyone, even people that I knew. Being in the choir was an ordeal, as on Sundays the long line of people passing through the Chancery on their way to take communion always looked at the choir boys. Whilst singing I was constantly flushed, with eyes down, making out I was reading the words of the hymns although I knew them all off by heart. At home, if any visitor knocked on the door, I would run upstairs. I couldn't face meeting, seeing or speaking to anyone. One day I intentionally drove a large nail through the skin between my thumb and index finger whilst hiding in one of the rooms at home. It didn't bleed much but what blood there was, I hid. I don't know why I did it, I suppose today, actions like this get described as 'self harm'. I must have been confused and unhappy.

I became increasingly insular and found comfort in music where I didn't have to look at anyone or speak to anyone. Those early songs I can remember now...... 'Green Door', 'Sixteen Tons', 'A White Sports Coat and a Pink Carnation', Alma Cogan, Frankie Vaughan, Perry Como and lots of others. I would sit alone with my ear to the radio singing along in my mind. The radio was pre-war, temperamental and very difficult to tune in. It had a ball and socket type of tuner that had to be carefully manoeuvred to the required position for your radio station, with little else to help you find the wave length you wanted. It was much like the gear shift lever in a car, with no slots to help you find the correct position. It had an 'accumulator' and it was my job to carry this heavy glass container filled with some kind of acidic fluid to the shop each week, to get charged up. The accumulator was left at the shop to be re-charged and a replacement was carried back to be fitted into the radio. The radio didn't last long after numerous complaints from my frustrated mother, who could not tune it in at all. My stepfather picked it up and dropped it out of the upstairs open window. I can imagine him saying "I won't have to hear you complaining about the radio anymore" and equally, I can imagine my mother saying "bloody good job it's gone." In the event, there was an almighty argument, a crash and there was no more music, no more radio serials such as 'Journey into space', 'Moby Dick' with Captain Ahab or, 'The day of the Triffids'. No more music either. Life would be unbearable now.

I don't know how, but I managed to acquire a very small crystal set and a pair of old earphones. The quality of this little radio was not very good and the volume was very low, but at least now I had my own music once again. I could be on my own lying on my bed enjoying 'my' music. I discovered a wavelength broadcasting Radio Luxembourg and this opened up a fantastic new world of music, much of which I had never heard of before. It was exciting, fresh and new and I found myself listening to Radio Luxembourg most evenings. Radio Luxembourg started later on in the evenings after regular serials such as 'The Archers' 'Journey into Space' and 'The day of the Triffids'. I don't know what would have happened if I had lost that little crystal set.

By now, our stepfather had become more of an object of ridicule than a surrogate father. My sister and I laughed at him and formed a bond of allegiance that he had great difficulty in breaking or entering. We despised his filter tips, tobacco and smell or the way he ate his food or slurped his soup. We were older. We had started to refuse his stupid sexual advances and his silly comments about keeping us in boxes to stop us growing up. The tide was turning but it created more arguments, tension and shouting in the home.

Still being acutely shy, I did not really have a circle of friends but just one or two whom I felt comfortable enough with to play marbles or cigarette cards. I had no one whom I could really talk to, but I had persuaded my stepfather to sign an HP agreement to buy a record player. It cost £5 with 2/6d for insurance. The agreement was signed in 'Berries' of Edmonton, a music company with branches of music shops all around London. The record player was second hand but I didn't care. It had an auto change and three speeds, 33, 45 and 78 rpm. What more could you want? I agreed in advance to pay the monthly HP payments out of my own money and decorated the record player with brightly coloured Fablon. The only record I had which was my very first that I had brought (even before having a record player), was 'Summertime Blues' by Eddie Cochran. This record was so good it got played over and over again on my new record player. It was played and worn so much that the black vinyl became white! It was the sound of the guitar and Eddie's voice. The sounds jumped out at you and could not be ignored. I only had this one record to play, but remembered the fun we had years previously at my Aunt Phyl's home with her old wind up record player and a pile of 78's. Music was fun. That memory and my own love of music convinced me that the £5 second hand record player was going to be a good investment.

The money for the record player was earned from my job that I had on Saturdays. I worked from 8.00am until 6.00pm at 'Sheltons', a greengrocers in St. Marks Road, Bush Hill Park. I thought I was quite well off earning 17/6d (85p) for my day's work. The job was actually quite hard work and involved continually filling up the vegetable bins with potatoes, carrots, cauliflowers and all of the other fruits and vegetables on display at the front of the shop. There was always a continuous line of customers queuing up for their shopping and so the bins needed to be filled every five minutes or so. The owner of the shop wanted to see us working continuously, although we did get to stop for a lunch break. He would shout out "carrots" or "King Edwards" and from the rear store room we would have to pile the necessary vegetables from sacks into a large sieve, carry them to the front of the shop and load up the bins. There were two of us young boys working in the shop on Saturdays, and one day we were in the store room at the back of the shop having our lunch break. The other boy had no lunch and was hungry. He took and started eating a banana whilst we were sitting down and the shop owner, Mr. Shelton, came out and saw him eating the banana. He pushed the whole banana down his throat nearly choking the boy. Mr. Shelton was not a very pleasant man and was later killed by his own vegetable lorry outside his shop. The lorry was jacked up to be repaired with Mr Shelton underneath effecting the repairs, it collapsed on him and killed him there and then in the road right outside his own shop.

I used to lie in bed for as long as possible leaving myself around five minutes to run around and get ready for work at 8.00am. It was around this time one Saturday morning that I was disturbed by my mother shouting up the stairs

"Rodney, get up – you've passed."

My bleary eyes opened,

"passed what?"

"Your exams" came the reply.

I'd forgotten that I'd even taken the 13 plus exam offered to children who had failed the 11 plus. Passing this exam meant nothing to me but trouble. I now had the choice of either going to Enfield Technical College or Tottenham Technical College. The only things I was any use at were drawing and listening to music. Tottenham Tech was chosen, as it was considered more appropriate for my 'artistic side'. I still don't know how that decision was arrived at, as the college specialised in building skills; plastering, brickwork, decorating, woodwork, plumbing and so on. Little did I know that the decision to choose Tottenham Tech would change my life forever.

I forgot about having to go to a new school and I continued with my relatively quiet life at Bush Hill Park. We were streamed at school and I found myself in the middle or 'B' group. The top pupils in each year who were the real 'brainies' went into the 'A' group. Kids with little outward sign of intelligence went into the 'C' group. If the teachers couldn't decide if you were stupid or brainy, they put you into the 'B' group. I never really took to school. I never realised its significance or the fact that it was supposed to be preparing you for adulthood and work. No one ever thought about going to universities in those days. School was quite a harsh experience, and there were various punishments meted out according to the severity of the crimes committed. If boys were caught fighting at playtime or during lunch break, the culprits would be pulled by the ear into the assembly hall and each given a giant pair of boxing gloves. All the kids would come in from the playground and form a large boxing ring sitting on the floor. The headmaster, Mr Skerman, would start the boxing match and the two young pugilists would take swings at each other for about 5 minutes. No serious damage was ever done and the pair would always finish off with a hug and a hand shake. I found myself in the ring one day and the gloves were so heavy I could hardly lift my arms to take a swing at my opponent. The technique that I discovered was to swing an arm at the opponent and if a connection was made, the weight of the enormous leather glove would knock them over. Many swings were made with very few actually connecting; it didn't really matter though. The adrenalin and energy were given their freedom and whatever started the fight was soon forgotten.

Pieces of chalk or blackboard dusters were missiles regularly used by teachers to test out their aim and accuracy against inattentive kids in the class. This could be quite dangerous, but it meant that you had to keep an eye on the teacher at all times, as sometimes the aim was not so good, and a missile aimed at someone else had to be avoided. I suppose it was actually quite a good way to make us pay attention. Girls were punished with smacks on the bottom. I remember seeing one poor unruly girl bent over the teacher's desk with her skirt hoisted up in front of the class, and her teacher giving her four good whacks on the backside with her hand. The girl was in tears. It was quite common to get the 'stick' or the 'cane' whilst having your name put in the 'black book', together with details of your misdemeanour. Mr Skerman, the head master, would administer the stick. He was a large man with possibly Nazi characteristics (assumed from his name and general manner) and had a small office in front of the school. I only went into that office on one occasion thankfully, and that was to receive my very own 'six of the best'. The event started in the music room where music lessons were given each week. The lessons which involved recorders (small flute like instruments), were boring and uninspiring and, to break the monotony of the boredom, one lad next to me decided to take apart a golf ball! I had no idea where he got a golf ball from, but watching him peel the white skin off and then start unwinding the layers of elastic inside the ball was more interesting than the music lesson. Quite a few of us were getting interested in the golf ball which was being unwound beneath the desk and out of sight of the teacher. Eventually, we saw a small rubber sack that was in the centre of the ball. The lad squeezed it and it burst showering white sticky liquid over 3 or 4 of us sitting by. We laughed out loud because it was very funny, but the teacher was not amused. She came over shouting, confused over what was going on and considered that there had been some kind of sexual activity.

The lad was told to clear the mess up and I was sent to the headmaster's office – I think the teacher believed that I was in some way responsible for what happened. The stick came out and I was told to hold one arm out and open my hand. I considered that if I lowered my hand just before the point of contact, the main impact could be avoided. It didn't work! The cane travelled faster than my reflexes. The headmaster hit me with the cane with all of his force taking a step forward and a large swing. Then he did it again on the same hand. I couldn't believe how painful it was. The whole thing was then repeated with my left hand and the red furrows of the cane's impact started swelling up straight away turning from bright red to white. Then I had to bend over his desk and receive two more lashes across the backside. I returned to the music room, holding my breath and biting my lip. I was crouching at my desk because it was too painful to sit down. A couple of the other lads close to me whispered

"Don't cry; don't let them see they've hurt you."

Tears were in my eyes, the tears came down, but I didn't cry.

There were only two classes during the week that I actually enjoyed and looked forward to; Art with Mr Quy and English with Mr Bailey. Mr Bailey was a very special teacher. He actually inspired us and taught us English without us really being aware of the fact that we were learning. He knew about music too and would be able to tune a guitar that someone had brought into the school. He would talk about music and get us to write about it. He was part of a group that investigated Atlantis – the lost city beneath the sea. He would talk about Atlantis and then bring in a tape recorder. None of us had ever seen a tape recorder before. The voice would come out of the tape recorder talking about Atlantis and we would listen, spellbound. Later on, we had to recall important parts of the story in our written essays. He would ask us about our ambitions and what we would like to become as adults. We had to write down our thoughts and then one by one have them recorded onto the tape recorder as we read out our own compositions. My ambitions were at that time to be a) a lion tamer or b) a spaceman. I always loved nature and wild life - particularly birds, and remember writing about the little owl (one of my favourite birds). The story had to be narrated and recorded onto the tape recorder and then listened to the following week during class. None of us liked listening to our own voices and consequently there was lots of giggling and even laughing out loud during this part of the class. Mr Bailey didn't mind this but always cleverly brought the class back to order to continue with the lesson. He talked about the 'Dead Sea Scrolls' and the impact that these recently found ancient documents may have upon religion and the Bible. We all loved listening to him, but he always made us write or do something to contribute to the lesson and our own education. Mr Bailey was an inspiring teacher and I can only thank him for the interest that I now have in writing and reading. In fact he was the only person in my whole school life who actually taught me anything that I find really useful.

My interest in ornithology was always strong, and this was manifest in my hobby of 'bird-nesting'. In the 1950s before it was made illegal, collecting birds eggs was my hobby and I would travel out to the country side on my bike with others who were similarly interested, to search for birds' nests and eggs. I didn't realise that this was not a very suitable way to conserve bird life, but I did only take one or two eggs from each nest so that the parent bird could continue incubating the remaining eggs and hopefully rear the young successfully. There was always something magical about finding a birds nest full of eggs; blue eggs for the hedge sparrow, white for the wood pigeon, brown speckles on blue for the blackbird, brown speckles on white for the robin or blue tit. I learnt a lot about birds and their habits and read old copies of the 'National Geographic Magazine' to cram my head full of bird information. I always had an affinity with birds and nature.

Skiffle music was coming into fashion and it created a lot of excitement at school. Word went round about 'washboards, broom handles and t-chests' and it wasn't long before everyone in the school knew about these new and unusual musical instruments which could actually be found in most homes. Some of the boys in school had guitars, and one by one, they would bring them to school to show off their skill at producing a rhythm in the key of E. A group of five or six boys used to get together in the playground during lunch break or playtime and strum along together. One day, a lad joined the group with a t-chest and a broom handle and then another brought a washboard and thimbles on his fingers. What a fantastic sound. The washboard provided the rhythmic clatter, as the fingers with the thimbles on, stroked and rubbed the metal washboard surfaces. The broom handle was attached to the t-chest with a length of string and then used as a lever to tighten or shorten the string while it was being plucked. This made the bass sounds whilst the guitars churned away on the chords of E, A or B7. Lonnie Donnegan was the hero of skiffle music, and it was his songs that the playground group used to try to copy. 'Rock Island Line', 'Lost John', 'Cumberland

Gap' and a few others sounded great in that playground. I so wanted to be part of it – part of the excitement – but I had no guitar and I was only a first year, a sort of non-entity to all of the older children and still covered in the spit stains as a result of my time in 'the pot'. The music and the rhythm were great to listen to, and more internal excitement was sparked off within me as I watched and listened to all of the different instruments being played in the playground.

One day at school, we saw the most unusual sight. We were all in the playground at a few minutes before 9.00am at which time we would file into assembly. A bright green and yellow car arrived at the school gates and out got one of the third year boys driven to school by his father. We were all clinging to the school railings with our mouths open looking in disbelief. One of the boys at school has a car! – not just any car but a shiny brand new car. It may have been a Vauxhall, a Zephyr or a Ford. No one was really sure, but that boy entered the playground like royalty. There were not many cars around in those days, in fact you were more likely to see a horse and cart than a car.

Cinemas were the hub of entertainment and social activity for young people. With exotic names such as The Savoy, The Rialto or The Florida in Enfield, or the Gaumont or the Odeon in Edmonton, these cinemas would draw us teenagers to them in groups, usually to try to 'chat up' a group of girls using a cigarette or two as 'bait', or to do a bit of 'snogging' in the back rows where there was not so much noise or interference. Girls in the front seats would often be annoyed with boys making such a noise behind them, and after turning around and shouting 'shut up', a conversation of jokes and innuendo would ensue with the boys eventually moving closer to the girls, sometimes jumping over a row or two of seats, to have a look and see whether the girls were worth a cigarette or two. I never really got the hang of this chatting up and wasn't too keen on cigarettes anyway. Being a little younger than most of those in my group, I remained on the outskirts of these events and enjoyed watching them as they unfolded. It was all pretty harmless fun but not so good for others who actually wanted to watch the film. It is amazing that there weren't more fires in cinemas, with matches and cigarette ends just being dropped on the floor or flicked across the rows of seats. One girl's hair did actually start smoking after a fag end was flicked and landed in her hair. We were all laughing and giggling behind her and then she turned round and saw the smoke, stood up and started screaming. The noise and disturbance to the cinema goers was often quite amusing and a shouting match would often break out between groups who wanted to watch the film and groups who were creating a disturbance. However I never saw any real violence or fighting in these situations. The attendant would march down the aisle, shining a big torch in the direction of the culprits who would be shamed into keeping quiet for a while. If there was too much of a disturbance, the culprits would be led out of the cinema protesting, by a couple of torch wielding uniformed cinema attendants.

The cinemas although sounding exotic, were far from it. Some cinemas were used by the lads to 'go a bit further' than snogging with their girlfriends, and these places usually showed more 'B' list kind of films – especially horror. The Florida in Enfield was one of these, and attendants went around regularly after performances with cans of DDT to kill off the ever reproducing resident fleas and vermin – hence the name the flea pit. I'm sure there were many of these infested cinemas up and down the country. We used to like seeing comedy films, horror films and, if possible, sexy films with Marilyn Monroe or Brigitte Bardot. I would not miss a Brigitte Bardot film, and always let my teenage fantasies go wild whilst watching these films. Amazing to think that you never actually saw a bare breast or any other actual nudity in any of these films. It was just the animal excitement of what might happen as the picture faded into another scene. 'And God Created Woman' was a Brigitte Bardot film that I just had to see. A group of us under-age lads went along and put on our most adult faces as we bought our tickets from the kiosk. In the foyer, there was a large Brigitte Bardot head and shoulders photo in one of the wall's picture frames. I had to have this and, when no attendant was looking, I prized the picture frame open, tugged the photo out and slid it craftily into my unbuttoned shirt. The photo looked down at me from my bedroom wall for a long time, igniting my passions and imaginations. It was a black and white head and shoulders shot, but that picture stirred my secret desires and my love of female beauty. I was probably one of thousands of young boys with Brigitte Bardot decorating the bedroom wall ready to be worshipped every night. I don't know how we got in to see 'And God Created Woman', it was 1956 and I was just 12 years old. Going to the cinemas or 'the flicks' was a great experience. It would often be daylight as you went in, and dark when the film finished and you came out. I would imagine being a character in the film as our group split up and we walked home in different directions. I used to enjoy the films for hours after they had finished – acting out in my mind a continuation of the story.

Cinemas were not just used for showing films. Sometimes, a wrestling ring would be erected in front of the screen area and the cinema would be given over to wrestling. I used to enjoy this and saw stars of the day such as 'Judo' Al Hayes, Mick McManus and the 'French Teddy Boys', throwing, punching and slapping their opponents around and often out of the ring. Karate had not really arrived, and we only got to hear about Judo, Jiu-Jitsu or of course wrestling, which I loved. Rock and Roll shows were often presented at the Odeon in Edmonton, and I saw stars like Chuck Berry, Jerry Lee Lewis, Duane Eddy, The Everly Brothers and Bo Diddely, all playing to packed houses when the cinema was given over to music. I don't quite understand how it happened, but these cinemas were gradually turned into Bingo Halls or supermarkets and then, one by one, closed down. The Odeon became a supermarket, The Florida was knocked down and became a road, The Rialto – one of the nicest cinemas I have ever been to – has just been demolished (2010) and is still awaiting development around thirty years after being closed. The poor old Rialto will probably end up as a car park, a supermarket or a block of council flats. The Savoy became a car park for a Tesco Supermarket. It's such a shame that all these wonderful old buildings which gave so many people so much enjoyment have now disappeared.

Having seen some of the musicians that came over and played in our local cinemas, I thought that I should have a guitar. In those days a guitar was not something you could go out and buy very easily, and so I used what I could find at home to make one. A broken tennis racquet and an old cigar box did the trick. I nailed the handle of the tennis racquet to the cigar box and used the gut from the weave of the racquet to make strings. It worked! I even got a few notes out of this rather strange looking instrument. I graduated shortly afterwards by trying to make a solid body guitar. When finished, I painted it white and hung it out on the clothes line in the back garden to dry - the neighbours thought it was a toilet seat hanging out there! I really wanted a guitar and if I couldn't buy one I would make one!

I had heard about electric guitars and realised that electric guitars had to have a 'pickup' (a special microphone that picks up the resonance of the metal guitar strings). I had seen pictures of electric guitars and one of the guitars that I had made at home was complete with strings and almost ready for use. I visited the local electrical suppliers, 'Berries' of Edmonton, and ordered a brand new 'Di Almond' pickup from their catalogue, at the price of £4.10s (around £4.50). One month later the pickup arrived and was quickly and excitedly screwed onto my home made guitar. Connected to the pickup was a cable that I considered must be plugged into the electrical supply to enable the guitar to become electric. I took the central and the outer wire from the cable and pushed one into the positive and one into the negative elements of the power socket on the wall. I switched the power on and waited. I heard a hum – it must be warming up I thought – I picked up the guitar; there was a blue flash and a crack of electricity. I put that smoking guitar down pretty quickly. I was shocked and annoyed. I took the burnt pickup back to the shop and complained that it must have been faulty.

"It's faulty and exploded." I argued.

"What kind of amplifier are you using?"

"Amplifier? I just plugged it into the mains socket."

A couple of disbelieving staff assured me that I was lucky to be alive and explained that an electric pickup or guitar must be plugged into an amplifier NOT the electrical supply.

I cant believe now that I actually DID this, but there was little in the way of information and help in those early days, unlike the world we live in today.

Music was my escape. The real world frightened me. People frightened me. My time at home would be spent alone in my bedroom with my music. In the safety of my cocoon, Songs like 'Reddy Teddy', 'Heartbreak Hotel' or 'Blue Suede Shoes', gave me an invisible friend and gave my life a secret meaning, something that was exotic, wild, and something that was mine whilst I mimed and danced alone in my room. The words from these songs were like no other, almost alien in fact, embedded into my mind together with every nuance, scream or shout that was there on the record. The excitement of playing or creating music like this overwhelmed me. Just listening to the music excited me so much. I couldn't believe that musical instruments were used to make these sounds, particularly the wild guitar on most of Elvis's records. The Rock n Roll music that I loved became a religion to me and I paid homage to it every night in my room. There was little chance to hear this kind of music on mainstream radio, the exception was Radio Luxembourg and later on the pirate ship Radio Caroline. Rock n' Roll demanded attention; it could not be ignored or used as background music. You had to listen, analyse, move or join in. Rock n Roll was medicine for the soul! When Christmas arrived there was only one thing I wanted - 'Elvis's Golden Records' - a collection of some of the best ever early Rock n Roll music. Somehow my Mum scraped the 30s (30 shillings - around £1. 50) together and got me the record. It came with a full colour picture book of Elvis in action and the album was played over and over again.

There were very few cars in those days, but you would often see a horse and cart going along the roads at home or outside the school. The 'rag and bone man' or the 'cockle and mussel man' would walk their horses slowly down the road shouting their trade mark call for business, a call which could never be really understood or translated into normal English - ('Ee ug o oh oh' is my nearest interpretation). It would not be long before the horse stopped, dumping a nice hot steaming pile of manure in the road and, after the horse started moving again, a nearby resident would be out there with a bucket and spade collecting everything that the horse had kindly left behind. There would also be seen a couple of other residents ready, standing in their doorways disappointed, bucket in hand. Talk about recycling. This must have been the quickest recycling ever. Horse eats straw, ejects it as manure, then manure goes onto the garden roses or tomatoes, all in the space of a couple of hours.

At other times the scrap merchant would be doing his rounds with a cart pulled by a giant long haired cart horse. 'Ee Eye O - oo' - translated as 'any old iron,' would be chanted every few yards, and residents would bring out anything old made of metal that they could barter for a few pennies or shillings. Finally, the cart horse got a rest, the merchant got his scrap metal and the resident got some cash to supplement the family budget. Everyone was happy and nothing was ever wasted.

Recycling, generally, in those days was quite natural for everyone. On the corner of each road there would be the 'pig bins.' Anything unusable that was left over from meals was taken and put in the pig bins. Potato peelings, old bones, stale or mouldy bread were all collected once a week from the pig bins and taken to the farms for the pigs to eat. The pigs were probably healthier in those days, eating actual food rather than chemical additives and processed feed. There was never much waste from each household, but together the residents of the road filled the pig bins each week ready for collection. This was another of my small chores "Rodney - can you take this over to the pig bins?" Clothing as well was passed from family to friends and vice versa – not worn out but grown out of, mended, and passed on.

Regular foods that we ate at home included smoked haddock which was cooked in milk, bread and dripping, bubble and squeak, sweetbreads, and once or twice, pig's trotters. The pig's trotters looked and smelt disgusting and I could not eat them. Rabbit was also difficult to eat whilst looking at the little legs and the remains of the carcass on the plate. Chicken was a rarity and only to be had at Christmas. After Christmas, the bones and skin would all be used to make a chicken curry and, the next day, anything left would be used to make chicken soup. One small chicken could provide meals for 3 days with some potatoes or rice. Preparation of the Christmas pudding was a tradition that I imagine all families followed. Two or three small silver coins would be included in the Christmas pudding mix and it was considered good luck to stir the mix before the pudding was cooked, and even better luck if you found one of these small coins whilst eating your bowl of Christmas pudding and custard. We would all take it in turns to stir the pudding mix before it was cooked, making a wish while we stirred the mixture. Curried eggs were also very nice. A boiled egg would be placed in a bowl of curry with some rice. Before the war, my father, whilst working in India as a typewriter mechanic for Remington, returned to England, enthusiastic about a local Indian dish – Curry. He brought back the recipe and hence we were probably one of the first families in England to eat curry on a regular basis. There were certainly no Indian restaurants in England in those days.

I did pick up some 'cooking' skills by being in the Cubs and later on in the Scouts. Here is my recipe if money ever gets scarce and you don't want to starve. This is how you make a 'Twist'

A handful of flour.

A cup of water

A straight preferably green twig from the garden

A spoonful of sugar or jam.

Strip the outer bark from the twig so that you have the smooth green inner part of the twig. Mix the flour and water so that you get a sticky kind of paste. Create a thick covering around the twig with this paste, leaving a length of twig for you to hold. Hold the finished twig and its covering over a flame and revolve it so that it gradually becomes brown and hard. When the mixture has become a nice even brown colour all round, pull it off of the twig (be careful not to burn your fingers). You now have a 'Twist'. Fill the hole in the centre where the twig was with sugar – or if you have it – jam. My sister and I used to have fun making these, making a mess and getting in our Mothers way.

'Hunters Stew' was another favourite that I learned to enjoy at Scout camp. A cauldron of boiling water would be hung over a raging camp fire. Everything available would be added to the bubbling water - carrots, turnips, tomatoes, parsnips, bacon, sausages, herbs, spices and even baked beans - everything would be thrown in and it would boil for around half an hour, (in much the same way as many of todays 'celebrity' chefs do in their own cooking demonstrations). The result would be lots of nice bowls of steaming food gobbled down by each of the young hungry Scouts sitting around the camp fire. On my return home I requested Hunters Stew from my Mother and received an incredulous look after explaining to her just how it was made!

CAPETOWN WARD
CHASE FARM HOSPITAL.

DEAR RODNEY
    I WAS VERY PLEASED TO GET YOUR LETTERS. AND I LIKED THE DRAWINGS VERY MUCH. I SHOWED THEM TO THE NURSES AND THEY SAID THEY THOUGHT THE DRAWINGS WERE JOLLY CLEVER.
    WELL, HOW ARE YOU KEEPING? I HOPE YOU ARE LOOKING AFTER MUMMY AND JANICE WHILE I AM IN HOSPITAL. I SHOULD THINK I SHOULD BE COMING HOME SOON BUT I DON'T KNOW WHEN. I EXPECT I WILL SEE THAT YOU HAVE GROWN A BIT TALLER WHEN I COME HOME. I GUESS JANICE HAS TOO. I HOPE HER COUGH IS GETTING BETTER.
    WELL, LOOK AFTER MUMMY

FOR ME AS SHE HAS A LOT TO DO NOW. AND SHE CAN DO WITH ALL THE HELP YOU CAN GIVE HER. I WONDER IF YOU WILL BE ABLE TO READ THIS LETTER BY YOURSELF?
    GOOD BYE FOR NOW
    FROM YOUR LOVING
        DADDY
        X X X X X X X

JANICE X X X X X X X
MUMMY X X X X X X X

CHANGE

'Feel the fear, and do it'

The day for leaving Bush Hill Park school and going to Tottenham Tech drew closer, and the closer it got the more petrified I became. In one sense I fitted in to Bush Hill Park and managed to deal with the trauma that took place on a day to day basis in my own personal way. Going to a new school would change all of this, and at 13 years old I would have to start again, not even knowing if going to Tottenham Tech was to be of any benefit. On top of that I did not know any of the other few boys who were moving to the same school from Bush Hill Park. I started to get more and more nervous and told my Mother that I didn't want to go to the new school.

The journey had been planned. I would catch the 8.15am train from Bush Hill Park station and get off at South Tottenham. From there I would take the 10 minute walk to the school. The train journey taking around 30 minutes would, together with the short walk, get me to school on time. I became more and more paranoid and tended to spend lots of time in my room away from everything and everyone. As the day for starting drew closer, I felt the panic in me swelling. On the actual day of the new school I had my long trousers (finally), my school tie and cap all in place. It was 8.00am and the train from Bush Hill Park would be leaving the station on its way to Tottenham at 8.15am. I could not go through with it. I sat down on a chair in the kitchen and would not – could not move. I wanted to die. My Mother was mortified and she was lost for words, not knowing just what to do or how to help me. I felt desolate, alone and lost. Even now, years later, I find it hard to understand why I was like this and why going to a new school was such a fearful experience. I had endured the fear of meeting people for so long and had managed to hide away in a kind of shell not to be noticed by anyone. The new school would change everything.

I ended up starting a few days later than everyone else, who by now knew their way around the school and had got to know a few friends and acquaintances and the names of the teachers. Their caps had gone and their ties were now skewed and I felt even more lonely than before. Everyone knew which lessons to go to and which classrooms to go to in the large campus that was divided up into different buildings and sections. Tottenham Tech was an all-boys college although there was a separate girls' department close by which we were never allowed into.

It came to light that us new recruits would spend a limited amount of time on each section of the syllabus and then choose which one we wanted to specialise in. A month in plumbing, then plastering, then decorating, carpentry, brickwork and so on. This was of course on top of the normal academic subjects such as Maths, Science, Art and English. My very first class was in Brickwork, a subject that I had no interest in whatsoever. I didn't really know what I was doing there or how I came to arrive at this awful place.

We were given overalls, trowels, sand, cement, water and a mortar board, and told to pair up. Most of the boys in the class had made friends and found it easy to find a partner to work with. I was alone; I looked around and there was just one short and rather strange looking boy left over for me to partner. "Thompson pair up with Butler" shouted the teacher, who was dressed like royalty in an immaculate suit, smart tie and a pair of shiny shoes that you could have eaten your lunch off of. I found out later that this was his style – his image, and he was generally a bit of a bastard who was known by the boys as 'Duke' or 'Dukey', and who could dish out the physical when necessary. We duly obeyed.

There was no messing about in 'Dukey's class, which seemed more like an army barracks than a school. We were taught how to mix the cement and then make a cement 'sausage' – this is the bit you put in between bricks to bond them together. Each boy had to take a turn to create a cement sausage on the mortar board and it was actually more difficult than it looked. I created what I thought was a pretty good sausage and then whack! Splat! Thompson's trowel came down and ruined it splattering cement everywhere. He had defied the general etiquette of the class and started mucking about! I considered this must be some form of jealousy and proceeded to studiously make another. The same thing happened again; splat! Then it was HIS turn to make a sausage. He looked quite proud of his sausage, but without even thinking, my trowel quickly came down on it and sent it to the sausage heaven in the sky. He tried again and once more my trowel found its target, this time showering wet cement over both of us. We both burst out laughing and were reprimanded (and probably mentally noted as well), by Duke. We enjoyed that lesson and I had made a friend – Bimbo, who probably was responsible for me eventually breaking out of my own home made prison.

You never can tell where these nicknames come from or where they originate. I found myself being called 'Snitch,' although it was a misnomer as I would and did never snitch on anyone. The name stuck, and throughout our short time at that educational establishment, we became popularly known as 'Bimbo and Snitch'. We became inseparable, missing lessons and skiving off together, nicking stuff from the local Woolworths or record store, comparing musical tastes and generally having a lot of fun.

Bimbo introduced me to a new world, a world of fun, laughter and mischief. We would listen to The Goon Show, mimicking the voices of Spike Milligan and Peter Sellers, or giggling, watch Popeye on the black and white television round at Bimbo's house in Church St Edmonton. Bimbo introduced me to the music of Buddy Holly, and listened in disbelief when told that I had not heard 'Peggy Sue', the new Buddy Holly record. The guitar sounds and the drums were different to the Rock n Roll that I knew. This music was unusual and more sophisticated than the music I had been listening to, but I soon came to love it and looked forward to each new record that was released every couple of months. These days were a revelation to me, and I gradually started to escape from the invisible cloak of fear and embarrassment that had clothed me for so long.

As well as Buddy Holly, we loved all of the music of that period; Eddie Cochran, Elvis Presley, Chuck Berry,

Little Richard, The Coasters, Jerry lee Lewis, Ricky Nelson, The Everly Brothers and loads more music imported and fed to us from the USA. We would sneak into the local café at dinner times, buying a coke or a cup of tea, to listen to the juke box being played, risking the punishment that would ensue if we were found by the school to have visited this banned and decadent establishment. Many of the local workers would have their lunch in this smokey little cafe in Tottenham high Rd and the juke box would be running non-stop. We could sit with a coke for nearly an hour listening to all of this great music, without having to put a penny in the juke box! Elvis singing 'Blue Suede Shoes' or 'Thats Alright Mama' seemed wild, untamed and in tune with my inner soul that was trying to escape. 'Yakety Yak don't talk back.' Rock 'n Roll was everything that my own life was not, and I wanted it.

The fashion was 'pegged' jeans; these were the normal fitting jeans that were tightened in each of the legs by using wooden clothes pegs to pull in the jeans at the bottom in order to narrow the leg. It was impossible to buy jeans with 12' leg width and so this is how some lads got those skin tight fitting jeans. It added a certain kind of 'panache' and daring to the wearer. Girls were impressed with this and some lads went to the trouble of wearing their pegged jeans underneath their regulation 18' bottom grey trousers at school. In the small park area adjacent to Tottenham Tech, boys and girls were free to mix at lunchtimes and so the lads who had the nerve to wear their pegged jeans underneath went off into a bush, whipped of their school trousers and became immediately more attractive to the girls who considered them more daring and dangerous than the boys wearing regulation school trousers. Naturally the school trousers had to be put on again before returning to the college. I never did any of this but watched and considered the ones who did it to be pretty hip kind of lads.

Another lunch time activity was pub crawling, not to partake of alcohol of course, but to swipe beer mats. Collecting beer mats was one of my hobbies, and during lunch times Bimbo and I would cover just about every pub within a mile or so radius of the college, nip in, swipe beer mats from the tables and be out again before anyone had a chance to catch and reprimand us. We had to be a disguised so that we would not be recognised as college students, and so the college jacket and badge would have to be removed for these illicit operations during lunchtimes.

I had an incredible collection of beer mats and received parcels of them from beer mat manufacturers in England. Tresises Drip Mat Company at Burton on Trent were particularly generous in sending dozens of samples after receiving a simple hand written letter from myself requesting beer mats. I found that breweries too would be happy to send me samples and wrote to breweries in England and abroad. The Amstel brewery in Holland sent some great beer mats and these were generally thicker and of much better quality than the English ones. One German brewer sent some very unusual beer mats; one had a miniature 78 rpm vinyl record impressed onto one side of the beer mat. The record could actually be played, and on my record player sounded like a German beer song which probably endorsed the brewers product. Some beer mats had raunchy pin up pictures of scantily covered girls on them, unlike the English rather more conservative advertising which featured things like 'Gourock Ropes', shipping lines, cigarettes, Swan

Vesta Matches and other boring products and services. If there was not much happening at lunchtime, Bimbo and I would do a tour of the pubs, running in to a bar, quickly nicking some beer mats from the tables, and then running out again before being caught. If we felt confident we would even casually go up to the bar and ask the barman if he had any beer mats to spare. 'For research' or 'for a school project' were the usual explanations that made the bar staff sympathetic to our requests. Collecting beer mats was actually more interesting than the lessons at school.

My collection of beer mats decorated my bedroom walls and almost covered the bland wallpaper and patches of plaster. There was no other way to display them all, and together with pictures of Elvis, Brigitte Bardot and a large print of Van Gogh's 'Sunflowers', the walls were completely covered, and redecorating just meant moving all of these items around into different positions on the walls. My bedroom became a bit of a novelty tourist attraction for many local friends who came round and who probably had proper wallpaper decorating their own bedroom walls.

Bimbo and I were both stunned in class when one winter morning the newspapers carried the story about the death of Buddy Holly, Ritchie Valens and The Big Bopper in a winter plane crash. We were in funeral mood for days after, not beginning to understand how something like this could happen. Pop music was so important to us all at that age. It formed the mood and the conversation of each of our days and seemed to describe our feelings, our frustrations and our youth. I brought my first record - 'Summertime Blues' by Eddie Cochran before I even had a record player! The rhythm, the words and the sound excited me and I still love that record and most of the other records that Eddie Cochran produced - especially C'mon Everybody and Twenty Flight Rock. We both considered the irony of Buddy's latest record release 'It doesn't matter anymore' as we loitered in local record stores listening stony faced to the record played over and over again.

We were complete opposites in many ways though. Bimbo was a natural sportsman – an athlete, he excelled at all sports and actually had a commodity that the school appreciated and found rather valuable; sporting success. It added to the schools reputation if, at inter school sports events, a student won an event or even made it to the finals. Bimbo actually won all of the swimming events that he entered; he could dive from the top board at Tottenham Lido and enter the water like an arrow after doing a summersault, a hand stand or back flip. Spectators gasped, teachers cheered loudly, everyone applauded, and Bimbo always marched off with a gold medal or a certificate. I hated water and could not swim but I did appreciate the skill of Bimbo and was pretty proud that he was my friend.

For Bimbo and myself the building skills that we learnt were often pretty boring. There was the occasional and punishable excitement of mischief, but the actual classes did little to stimulate me. We were told in no uncertain terms to keep water away from the large pot of molten lead in the plumbing class. One lad decided to find out why, and dropped a cupful of water into the cauldron of boiling lead. There was an explosion and molten lead shot up and onto the ceiling and splattered everyone's clothes making lots of little burn holes. Later on, after the lead had dried, it remained on the ceiling.

No one was actually injured but I never saw that lad again in the plumbing class.

There was but one occasion to escape the tedious monotony and the danger of classes; a school day trip out. We were taken to a plasterboard factory. A place which British Gypsum owned and manufactured plasterboard! The coach was secretly loaded with cans of beer and fags, adequately disguised as bags of homework and off we went, no interest in plasterboard or gypsum, but a great interest in drinking beer behind the teachers back and having fun outside of the confines of school. I refuse to even call the place a college.

All of the teachers had nicknames and by far the weirdest one was 'Bruno' or Mr. Brunsdon. He was the chemistry and science teacher and I cannot begin to understand why on earth he chose his occupation as a teacher. He was quite an ugly man - strangely grotesque, which didn't help his career as a teacher. His face was virtually covered with moustache, eyebrow and beard hair. He had a lisp and a rather large lower lip that protruded out from his hirsute face. His bulbous eyes bulged and when he talked he showered the area with spit, consequently we all stayed pretty clear of him and well out of range. He had no control over the class and as fast as he chalked up scientific data onto the black board, we rubbed it off when he was distracted or when he left the room. There were often flames, smoke and bad smells in that laboratory, 'accidents' created by the boys, and we all laughed at the poor man's resulting frustration, lisp enhanced shouting complete with showers of spit, and finally, his anger. He would send boys out of the laboratory for misbehaving and sometimes there were more students outside in the corridor than there were in the laboratory. One particular boy was marched out by the scruff of the neck; there was a scuffle in the corridor and some screaming and shouting. Bruno was on the floor with the boy straddling him punching him in the face. We had to pull him off and Bruno had to go to hospital. We heard that the boy's parents were written to about the incident and were requested to visit the school with their son. The story goes that the parents would only attend the school enquiry if their son was not punished. He never came back to school.

It was tough, no doubt about it. I was punched in the face and knocked down by a teacher in one of the 'lessons'. No particular reason, but the teacher had a few of us around him and he just let rip. I staggered out of the classroom to find the principle of the college - 'Jock' Mc Gregor. He was sitting down taking a lesson in one of the class rooms. I made my complaint to him expecting him to go to the teacher concerned. He opened the drawer in his desk and pointed to a very large knife saying "We get a lot of trouble here, go back to your class." That was my experience of justice at Tottenham Technical College. It was an awful school and the only thing that I learnt was how to survive.

Sports and in particular PE were enthusiastically promoted by the school. I imagine it gave the teachers a break from the difficulty they had in teaching us. At the end of each PE lesson we had to take showers. This was the first time I had taken or even seen a shower. There was a long tiled cubicle with around twenty shower heads and we all had to strip off and wash ourselves in the tepid water. What was the point? I was not even sweating. I had never seen so much male nudity; all shapes all sizes. Unbelievable! Some long like elephants trunks hanging down, some almost non-existent covered by a mass of hair – loads of it! Where was my hair? Most of these boys had hair sprouting from everywhere, particularly from under the arms, the upper lips and around the pubic area. I had nothing to speak of, just a few wisps, barely mentionable. You couldn't help but look, but no one else seemed to be looking – only me. Of course there were a few slackers – lads who had been slow in running around the circuits in the PE gym or slow in making their way through the shower; red marks on the backside, large shoe shaped marks where the teachers Gym shoe had landed. In the gym or in the showers you couldn't escape the sports master's shoe landing hard on your backside.

I hated all of this exercise and in particular I hated the showering and the slipper on my backside and so a plan was devised. I often suffered from nose bleeds; a weak blood vessel in one of my nostrils. My friend Bimbo assisted me with the plan by kindly giving me a swift knock on the nose before these PE lessons. The nose would start bleeding and I subsequently had a suitable amount of blood around my nose and on my handkerchief to be excused from the lesson. The plan worked and was introduced on a regular basis. Great! I didn't have to do those stupid lessons, running around and jumping over the ridiculous apparatus in the gym. Given the choice, who would really want to jump over a wooden 'horse'? After a few weeks of missing these classes with blood all over my face, the teacher seemed to realise that I was a 'no hoper' in the gym and I was excused regularly. After a while, I didn't even have to have the nose bleeds, I just pointed to my nose and was waved out of the gym. Clever or What?

Bimbo and I devised further ways to escape from the school when we wanted or needed time off. We invented excuses such as a doctor's appointment, a feigned injury or a dentist's appointment. They all worked – for a while, but then after various teachers became suspicious, we had to provide evidence. We didn't let the demands for evidence deter us. Bimbo actually did have a real dentist appointment and returned to school triumphant with a nice pile of dental appointment cards nicked from the surgery. We were laughing our heads off; these cards were worth more than their weight in gold. Apart from escaping school when we wanted to with a card indicating an appropriate time, the cards could be sold or bartered to other lads who needed to get away for a morning or afternoon.

Cross country running was compulsory. It was just a few miles running around Tottenham marshes. Of course I hated it (together with quite a few others), but we had to do it. There were ways to shorten the run and one of them was to sneak along on your knees behind a block of tennis courts. This virtually halved the circuit of the run, but bugger me if the teacher in charge started to bring along a pair of binoculars to catch the lads sneaking behind the tennis courts. It was easier to get a 'nose bleed' or a 'dentist appointment' than to sneak through those tennis courts.

Important lessons which were given to more than one or two classes at the same time were given in the large lecture theatre. The lecture theatre had sloping seating leading down to a presentation stage with a desk and a film screen on the wall. High above the film screen was large clock, and on this particular day we were waiting for a lecture to begin. The minutes went by and it was clear that the lecture would start late and finish late. There were important things that a couple of us wanted to do, and so I devised a plan; if one lad stood on the desk and I climbed up and onto his shoulders I could reach the clock, move the hands forward by half an hour and hopefully shorten the lecture when it actually did begin. One lad stood on the desk; I climbed onto his shoulders and stretching up could just about reach the clock. There was a small knob under the clock that had to be pushed up and turned to move the hands around. I pushed the knob up and the hands started turning, and then the clock slowly tipped forward and very noisily crashed to the floor below. Glass and the intestines of the clock were strewn across the floor. At that moment the teacher walked in. He was fuming. "Just putting the clock right sir." My comment didn't work but seemed to make the teacher even angrier. I had the normal interview at the principles office and was told that my association with Thompson had influenced my behaviour and my association with him in college had to stop! I refused to end the association and my friendship. Bimbo together with his parents had the same kind of interview and he was told that his association with me had to stop; I was a bad influence on him. He also refused. We were both told not to apply for a further year at the college and, in effect, we were expelled. Fifteen years old and what freedom, what fun we could have now that we were free of this awful place. We did. Together with our bikes and catapults, we got slug guns (air guns), and had great fun in the woods of Broxbourne shooting at each other (and anything else that crossed our path). Bimbo and Tottenham Tech were the catalysts that offered me an alternative character and personality to the shy and introverted one that I previously had. I liked the new person that I was changing into and liked the fun that could be had.

Bimbo had moved to Broxbourne. Compared to my family Bimbo had a family that was quite well off. The family lived in a nice large detached country house situated close to the New River *and* with a home telephone. I would be a regular visitor, travelling to his house on my bike at weekends, riding through Enfield, Waltham Cross and Cheshunt and on to Broxbourne. During the week, we communicated either by letter or telephone. Letters were easy enough to send but the telephone was a different matter. Our home did not have a telephone and subsequently I had no idea of how to use one. There was a public telephone box quite near to our home and on inspection, I found that inside the red telephone box, there was a large black contraption with the telephone sitting proudly at the top. Money had to be inserted, and there were two large silver buttons - one on the side and one on the front of the big black box - button 'A' and button 'B'. I had no idea how all of this worked, and explained to Bimbo in a letter that it would be best for us to communicate by letter in future as the telephone box was impossible for me to use. By return I received written details and a hand drawn diagram describing just how to make a telephone call from the local box. The instructions worked but it seemed very strange to hear a voice coming from the telephone receiver. I never felt comfortable using that telephone and still don't like them even today.

SHOCK

'You don't know where your next square meal is coming from' – My Mum.

I f you are not going to school or college, you're not going to laze around here!

My Mother's voice sounded harsh and I knew I had to get a job. Aged fifteen, I was sent to the employment office to look for employment. I wanted to be an artist but was told there were no jobs available for artists. What else would you like to do? Well, at Tottenham Tech there was a lesson called 'Technical Drawing' and although I hated the school and its teachers, I did get some kind of artistic satisfaction from this lesson. I explained that I would be happy to take a job doing technical drawing and was sent for an interview at CESCO – The Car Electrical Service Company! The business was based in London Rd Enfield and is now a petrol station. At 15 you know nothing. I did the interview and was offered the job as assistant to the service manager on a wage of £3/5 shillings a week (around £3.25). Reading the small print I had missed out two small but very important words in the job description; 'to the.' I was to be not an assistant manager but an assistant *to the* manager Mr Kerly, a jolly, short and rotund human dynamo. No technical drawing whatsoever was involved in the job. I had to support Mr Kerly the service manager by answering the telephone, creating invoices and preparing items such as starter motors, trafficators (indicators), dynamos, regulators and all sorts of electrical equipment for dispatch. It was a novelty going to work, but it was quite difficult to get used to the early 8.30 in the morning start and the 5.30pm finishing time, much longer than the 9.00am to 4.00pm school day that I was used to. I picked up the job requirements and skills quickly, and after a few months I realised that I was actually doing the service managers job and running the office more efficiently than him. I was always working and never sat around with nothing to do. I always found work to do, such as tidying the stock bins, filing the invoices, helping out in the service department stripping down dynamos and starter motors, or chasing up supplies that had not arrived. I got on Mr Kerly's nerves by finishing my jobs quickly and then asking him for another job. I was bored with nothing to do, although a lot of the other employees didn't mind this and often just stood around talking or telling jokes when jobs had been completed. Everything came to an abrupt stop at 1.00pm – lunchtime. If it was sunny, we would sit outside eating our sandwiches and drinking tea. More often than not it was raining and so a group of us used a derelict unused room in the loft of the building where six or seven of us would play cards and exchange jokes during our lunchtime. Being cold and miserable, we wanted something warm to eat so we took it in turns to use the electric fire. The two bar electric fire was turned onto its back and used to make toast or warm our sandwiches up. Sparks and flames would often shoot up as food dropped or melted onto the red hot elements of the fire. It was amazing that the building was not burnt down by this dangerous lunchtime habit. I used to cycle to and from work carrying my bike over my head across the railway line in Lincoln Rd, which I used used as a short cut. I saw plenty of motorbikes at work and really fancied getting a motorbike to improve my mode of transport. I loved the sound of them, the smell and the power.

There was always some fun to be had at Cescos, especially when a new lad started in the repair shop. The initiation of the new employee included being pinned down and a large handful of 'Gunk' – a thick green jelly like substance used for cleaning oil from hands – thrust down the inside of the trousers of the new recruit, front or back! Luckily, me being in the office and not in the workshop, I never had to endure this somewhat humiliating tradition.

I decided that I was worth more than £3/5s a week and asked Mr Kerly for a rise. He seemed shocked and said he would have to put my request in front of the board of directors. He explained to me that this may take some time and so I decided to forget about it for the time being. I asked again a few months later if there was any news of my wage increase. "No news. The directors are still considering the matter" came the abrupt reply. I asked again a few weeks later and was told "Good news. The directors have decided to increase your wages. You will now be getting £3/7/6d a week" (around £3.35). I was disappointed. I thought I might be getting a little more, but not showing my disappointment thanked him, and showed him my appreciation for his efforts.

Music was and still is a great motivational force in my life and in the 1950s and 1960s there was a shop that all young people gravitated to called 'Saville Pianos' (HMV in Enfield and latterly another supermarket). This was the one and only record shop in Enfield Town and, as well as selling records, it sold sheet music and various musical instruments as well as record players and radiograms. Saville Pianos had a monopoly of music shops throughout London, and the Top Ten must have been based on the records that they sold throughout the week. I finished work at CESCOs at lunchtime on a Saturday, and my usual habit was to ride down to The Town and have a look in Saville's and listen to some of the latest music. One Saturday whilst looking in the window, I saw one of the shop assistants cellotaping a small piece of paper inside the glass front window. When the shop assistant moved away I looked at the small notice. SHOP ASSISTANT REQUIRED – ENQUIRE WITHIN. My heart raced. Could I? Should I? I tried to look confident and went in, leaving my bike outside leaning against the window. An interview was required and I had to attend the following Monday at 10.00am to be interviewed by the manager for the job. I could not contain my excitement and decided that I had to have the job no matter how much money I was to be paid.

I got out my smartest clothes, a clean shirt and of course a tie. The interview was quite simple. I was asked my name, address, age and a few other easy questions. I didn't ask about the wages but was told that I would be getting £3/17/6d. I couldn't believe my luck. I was going to work in a record shop and get more money than I ever thought possible, certainly more than I was getting at CESCOs. I went home ecstatic, but my Mother was more cautious, questioning whether it was right to leave the job that I had been trained to do. I was dreading telling

Mr Kerly. I had to give two weeks notice and of course he was angry, saying that he had wasted his time and effort training me to be a service manager's assistant. I felt rotten about it but knew that I was doing the right thing – well, the right thing for me anyway. Saville's here I come! Those two weeks seemed like two years and I knew my life was changing direction.

At this point we moved house. An opportunity arose for the family to move into a large house in Wellington Rd (quite a posh part of Enfield), and live there rent free, acting as caretakers for the premises. The lower part of the house was in fact a synagogue used by the local Jewish community for their meetings and worship. The upper part of the house formed our family accommodation and very nice it was too. My sister had her piano installed in the lounge and I had my beer mats and record sleeves installed as decoration on the walls of my own bedroom, which looked out across the large rear garden and onto the local tennis club courts. A new three piece suite was purchased from 'Courts' in Palmers Green; a new twin tub was installed for my Mum; my stepfather acquired a newish car and he would polish it and generally take care of it as if it was another member of the family. I don't know where all the money came from to pay for such luxuries but there was a general air of excitement that things were going well for us. Friends generally joked about us living in a synagogue and our home was christened and generally known as 'The Syn'.

The job at Savilles was not quite as glamorous as I originally thought. I had to hump the iron security bars and gate out in the morning and in again at night, unlocking it all in the morning before 9.00am when the shop opened and locking it all up again at night. Pianos and radiograms had to be dusted and polished every day. Floors had to be swept and rubbish put outside for the dustmen. Deliveries had to be unpacked and checked. When the chores were finished I could join the other staff behind the counter as a shop assistant. Every day I watched as the customers were served by the staff, and one salesman particularly impressed me. A customer would ask for a certain record and to find it, the number of the record had to be known or looked up in the Gramophone directory. Ron, a very confident member of the counter staff, knew the number of every record, and if a customer asked for an LP, EP or single, he would know the number and go straight to it in the rows of stock behind the counter. It was amazing to see him work and amazing to see how he remembered the numbers of so very many records.

I had never actually served anyone myself. I found the idea of actually talking to a stranger extremely frightening. If I found myself in a situation where I might have to initiate contact with a customer, I would find a job to do out back in the stock room, unpacking orders or bundling up cardboard to be collected. This went on for a couple of weeks and after a period of time my actions were noticed and I was asked why I never served any customers. The game was up. I had been discovered; although I never could admit that it was my shyness that stopped me serving customers. I decided that in order to keep the job I had to serve at the counter like all of the other staff. In front of everyone, and before anyone could jump in before me, I seized the opportunity to serve. "Can I help you sir," I blurted out in a rather shaky voice. "I would like a copy of The 1812 Overture please" came the reply. I looked to Ron – the human record number encyclopedia – and he quietly told me the number. I went to the shelf, found the record, inspected it for dust or scratches, wrapped it in a Saville's bag, took the money, gave the change and a big sigh of relief, as the happy customer left the shop. The other staff looked at me with pride and smiled as if I had just won the lottery. I felt good!

After that it became much easier to serve customers or answer questions. Giggling girls in groups would always come in on Saturdays. During the week it was older customers during the day and younger customers after 4.00pm when the schools closed. Most of the after 4.00pm customers wanted to listen to records or hang around and talk in the shop. One day Cliff Richard came into the shop with his Mother to listen to and buy a record. Naturally the Under Manager of the shop had to serve him, we all watched, craftily taking note of everything said and done. Cliff Richard was quite a star with hits such as 'Move It', 'Living Doll' and 'Travelling Light' at that time. We were all buzzing with excitement.

One of the benefits of opening the shop in the morning was seeing other shops being opened at the same time. The shop on the opposite side of the road to Saville's in Church St was Boots the chemist (now a book shop and prior to that a shoe shop). Boots was always opened in the morning by a very pretty girl who gradually started smiling at me as we both opened our shops. Every morning in my black suit and tie I would get a nice smile or a wave and I used to look forward to seeing her. The smiling and waving went on over a period of a few weeks and one day one of the other girls from Boots came into my shop. She asked me if I would like to make up part of a group who was going out for a day to Southend.

I agreed to go, and finally met Maureen Smith who I saw every morning at 9.00am opening Boots, but who I had never actually met or spoken to. Still pathologically shy, I managed to make a nice friendship with Maureen and we went out quite a few times. I visited her family in Upshire and got to know the timetable for the buses from Enfield to Upshire pretty well.

I was new to the boyfriend/girlfriend thing and didn't really have much idea of how this kind of relationships worked. When it came time for Maureen to go on holiday for two weeks with her parents, I was quite upset as I was going to miss not seeing her or going out together. Maureen could see this and told me not to mope about but to go out and have fun with other friends. She was a fun kind of girl and I took the words literally, dating a couple of other girls while she was on holiday. We met up as soon as soon as she returned and we exchanged pecks, holding hands, kisses and all of our news and gossip. After Maureen had told me all of her holiday stories she asked me what I had been doing. I explained that one evening I had taken Valerie to the pictures and another day I had met up with Doreen for a walk in the park. She went mad! I explained that it was just fun to stop myself feeling miserable but that was it. She jumped on a bus and was gone.

I did not handle this very well and decided the next day to wait for her outside the United Dairies (now a wooden pallet store) in Waltham Abbey where she was now working. She knew I was waiting for her and I saw her sneak away craftily onto a bus to escape. I ran to catch the bus. I ran as fast as I could but could not catch the bus up. At that point I saw a United Dairies milk float leaving the dairy and heading in the same direction as the bus. I ran into the road waving my arms and told the driver to follow that bus – "It's a matter of life or death" I shouted. He let me cling on to the side of the milk float and eventually, over bumps, hills, twists and turns he caught up with the bus, Maureen jumped off, ran for her home and ran indoors slamming the front door. I shouted "stop" to the milk float driver and was hence abruptly thrown from the milk float. I picked myself up ran to her house and banged on the door. I waited and waited but she wouldn't come to the door, and so that was the end of that romance. I never saw her again. I was not ready for a girlfriend and I certainly did not understand girls.

From that peak of social and romantic success, my relationships with girls continued on an ever downward spiral. I considered that for a girl to be interesting she had to have a bike or at least have an interest in bikes. If a girl could point out the brake shoe, the lugs or the valve on a bike there was an instant and unstoppable attraction. I had a Dayton bike with a Sturmy Archer three speed gear change and custom 'cow horn' handlebars. Most girls I knew did not have bikes and most were quite bemused to see me arrive at their homes for a 'date' on my rather unusual bike. There would be even more surprise when I invited them out for a ride on the cross bar. Valerie Sawyer and Jennifer Ferris particularly were regulars on my cross bar, and both seemed to enjoy the experience. Of course I realise now that this is not exactly what young ladies see as a guide or signal to the possibility of a good future relationship, but I did not really understand the requirements of young ladies, and actually considered that they were pretty cool coming out with me and riding on my cross bar. As you can no doubt judge, I was a late developer and my criteria for a

good girlfriend was that;
1. She had to be good at wrestling
2. She had to have a bike or be prepared to go out on the crossbar of my bike.

I was not good boyfriend material, but the girls I knew did not seem to mind (well at least most of them that is). My bike was very important to me in those days; I was mobile, independent, I could go anywhere and not have to rely on buses or trains.

Let me describe another of my doomed relationships. I always had an interest in war, explosives and guns. I actually made a gun and successfully fired it in my back garden. A small steel tube with a hole drilled in the side was blocked at one end. Gunpowder from fireworks was used as the explosive and an old bullet (most boys owned a few bullets left over from the war) was used as the projectile. I held the 'gun' in a vice outside in the garden and ignited the explosive using a small fuse taken from a firework. A tremendous bang and clouds of smoke followed and I found that the bullet had gone straight through the metal dustbin, which I had used as a target, and out of the other side. The dustbin was full of rubbish and so I have no doubt that the bullet could have actually killed someone. I was rather shocked and didn't carry that kind of experiment any further. I did however, get hold of a starting pistol. The pistol used blank rounds, which when fired were very loud and always caused panic and a commotion. At this point I had a new 'girlfriend' – Doreen Prosser - well not really a girlfriend but a kind of 'mate'. She was blonde and extremely pretty. We got on quite well and we often resorted to wrestling, in much the same way as boys do. We often argued and had these bouts of wrestling or arguing in public or in the park, often finishing up in fits of laughter. At the time this was my idea of a promising relationship. However, one evening we were out with a group of other young boys and girls generally having fun and making a lot of noise with the boys trying to impress their mates and the girls. The arguing started between myself and 'Pluto' (the nickname for my girlfriend). We started pushing and shoving each other and neither of us would back down. I pushed her onto her backside into a low hedge, took out my starting pistol and shouted;

"Right, that's it, you are going to die!" - I pointed the gun at her and fired.

There was a flash and a loud bang, everyone screamed and Pluto shouted;

"You bastard!"

I was laughing at the spectacle – "I didn't mean it - it was only a joke."

We didn't see much of each other after that. It took me many years before I started to understand girls. Even now as an adult, I find it difficult to understand the female of the species and the joy and happiness that is derived by the opposite sex from buying just a handbag, another pair of shoes or earrings.

I was still working in Saville's and loved the job and the perks. Naturally one of the perks enabled staff to play the new records that arrived before anyone else had heard them. As well as playing the new records, I discovered other forms of music and other artists that interested me greatly. I always loved guitar music and listened to jazz, country, and blues guitarists whenever I got the chance. I started listening to the jazz of the MJQ, Dave Brubeck, Miles Davies and eventually the great Wes Montgomery. I was introduced to the music of the legendary Chet Atkins by one of the staff who knew of my passion for the guitar. I purchased all of his records that were available starting with the album 'Teensville' and I eventually got hold of many American imports that were not widely available. In the following years I visited many venues and saw loads of artistes that I originally discovered in my job at Savilles. Ella Fitzgerald, Count Basie, Wes Montgomery, Barney Kessel and of course Chet Atkins. Various venues hosted these events; Ronnie Scotts Jazz Club, The Royal Festival Hall and lots of other theatres and clubs in London's West End. The seed had been planted and my passion grew. Out of the blue one day one of the Jewish worshipers at the 'Syn' showed me two tickets for a concert at Hammersmith Odeon. The two tickets had been bought for someone that couldn't go to the concert. Face value of around £2 was required and the show was - The Beatles! I grabbed the tickets and quickly obtained the money to pay for them. The sellout show was the next day and so when it was time to leave, my Sister and I jumped into my old Austin 7 (just purchased for £10 after passing my driving test) and headed off on the North Circular Rd towards Hammersmith. At Finchley Rd the brakes failed and so I had to drive at minimum speed to the venue just using the hand brake to slow down or stop.

The Beatles of course were brilliant; only playing for what seemed like 45 minutes with girls screaming constantly while the music played. I seem to remember Sandie Shaw and Micky Most supporting the Beatles but nobody was there to see either of those two rather boring acts, everyone was there for The Beatles.

Of course working in this job at Savilles where I had to deal directly with the public was beneficial to me in many ways; I had to overcome my shyness and be able to integrate into the world more successfully. The job did that, and together with the last couple of years at Tottenham Tech, I found I could control these feelings of shyness and insecurity or at least replace them with a facade of confidence. I enjoyed my new found freedom and confidence but realise now that this was a shell that I hid beneath.

Whilst working at Saville's I met like-minded people who were also interested in guitars and groups. One of these was Roy Green who worked for the local council in the horticultural nurseries. He was often in and out of the shop listening to records (but not buying any) and I discovered that he was actually the drummer in a band based in a district that was then a hotbed for new young rock talent; Cheshunt in Hertfordshire. Even more interesting was the fact that his band was looking for a guitarist as their original guitarist had decided to leave. I was intrigued and found out that the band was going to hold auditions at the singers home. My enthusiasm was in greater supply than my skills as I must have had a surge of confidence (and stupidity); I told Roy that I was a guitarist and that I would be interested in joining the band! As we had formed quite a friendship always talking about music, bands and records, he invited me to come along for the audition. I went by bike along to the house in Chestnut and met the band members including Roy the drummer.

I was asked where my guitar was and what make it is.

"I don't actually have a guitar at present as I have sold my old one and am getting a new one" came the lie.

An acoustic guitar was found for me to play and

of course I was totally embarrassed as I was holding the guitar the wrong way round and couldn't play a thing. One of the band members suggested that I must be left handed, and so that became my excuse for not being able to play anything on this right-handed guitar. Relieved I put the guitar down. I was not to escape the humiliation however, as another of the band members suggested that I take the strings off and re-string the guitar for a left handed player, something of which was way outside of my capabilities. I was going a deeper and deeper shade of red, and at this point the band asked me to wait outside whilst they have a 'meeting'. After a few minutes my friend Roy came out of the room and announced that he was quitting the band. I came clean and apologised to him for lying. I explained that I had no guitar, I could not play and that I wanted to apologise to the band for wasting their time. Roy had had an argument with the other band members as he wanted me to be given a chance and the others, quite naturally, did not want me involved in any way, shape or form. Against all of my wishes he did leave the band and I then made plans to actually get hold of a guitar.

This period of time from the age of 16 to 19 contained the elements that formed the next 20 years or so of my life. I wanted nothing more than to be able to play the guitar. I felt as if the music was inside me and it needed to escape. The sounds were in my head but I had no idea how to create them. Unlike today, there were no videos or self help documentaries from which to learn, the only thing available was a small brown booklet called '*Bert Weedon's Play in a Day*' guitar tutor, which showed the basic chords and the tunes to put them to. I had experimented with making guitars and had made friends with anyone who owned a guitar of any description. I was totally naive – some would say insane or stupid – and that naivety has followed me throughout my whole life. I have got used to it now and enjoy the freedom of thinking and the creativity that it gives me. However, I do get labeled with the term 'too trusting' or 'daft' quite often. The guitar, the Rock n Roll, the music, meant freedom; uninhibited and wild freedom, and it has always excited me and drawn me towards it.

After my previous, unsuccessful and disastrous attempts at trying to make guitars, I decided to try to locate a guitar supplier who could provide me with a real (and safe), left handed electric guitar. I actually had a desire to get a motorbike as well, but the general consensus and advice was 'get a guitar - it's safer!' I discovered 'Charlie Footes' at Denman St, in London's West End, a retailer of various kinds of musical instruments and an agent for Burns guitars. There were quite a few music shops in London but very few stocked electric guitars and 'Footes' was the only shop which could get hold of a left handed guitar. The shop agreed to order me a 'Burns Artiste' custom made, cherry red, left handed electric guitar for the astronomical price of £107.00. £20 was required for the deposit and I had to persuade my stepfather to sign as a guarantor for the agreement as I was too young to sign (under the age of 18). After lots of family discussion and arguing he reluctantly agreed. I never missed a monthly payment to the hire purchase company. £3/19/7d was paid into the post office every month until the debt was cleared. The amount is indelibly inscribed into my mind.

After 6 months my new Burns guitar arrived, shining and polished and waiting to be played. Of course I still had no idea of how to play it and soon realised that

I had no money left to buy an amplifier for the guitar. I decided to try to make a budget amplifier and purchased a 10" x 8" elliptical loud speaker and a small hi-fi amplifier unit. These items together with some wood, wires and plugs became my first ever amplifier, and covered in 'Fablon' (coloured adhesive plastic), looked great! After all of the wiring up was completed it was time for a test run. To my surprise the amplifier and the guitar actually worked and the volume of the small hi-fi unit was actually pretty good. The small elliptical speaker was overloaded when the amplifier was turned up and it gave me a slightly earthy distorted sound. The cheap little hi-fi amp was made by an Italian company called 'Dulci' and as I had designed and built the cabinet that contained everything, I called my amp the 'Dulci-Butler'. It gave me a great sound - earthy and slightly distorted. I attached the letters RB to the front of the cabinet, considering that I wouldn't have time to do this when I became famous!

Roy Green and myself practiced together almost every evening in the canteen at Enfield Rolling Mills at Brimsdown. His Dad worked there and when the canteen was closed at night time we had access to practice there and make what must have been an awful noise. We travelled to the Rolling Mills on our bikes; Roy with his drum set strapped around him and me with my amp strapped to my back and my guitar case strapped to the crossbar of my bike. We made friends with another guitarist who actually had a guitar (and unlike me could also tune it). He was encouraged to join our 'band' and because he could actually play the guitar I could pick his brains and learn from him. This guitar player who was much older than Roy or myself, taught me the chord structure of many songs explaining that although all songs were different there was often a basic common chord structure relating many songs that could be picked up quite easily. Roy had an Olympic drum set and I had a Burns guitar. We called ourselves the 'Burns Olympic 4' and began events that would shape my musical life for the next 20 years.

Our first ever 'gig' was in the St Marks Church hall on the corner of Millais Rd where I used to live. It was a Scouts and Guides social event with table tennis, darts and various other games. I had miraculously managed to learn a couple of instrumental numbers including 'Hoolie Jump' by Jim Gunner and 'Guitar Boogie Shuffle' by Bert Weedon, and these were repeated over and over again during the evening. The three of us wore our brightly coloured waistcoats made for us by Roy's Mum. These waistcoats were our band uniform and we must have looked pretty impressive with our white shirts, black trousers, black ties and bright orange waistcoats. At the end of the evening Mrs Gabriel (who lived next door at number 5 Millais Road) came over on behalf of the committee and thanked us for our efforts.

"We don't have any money to pay you but please accept this as a thank you". She gave us a one pound note to share between us and we were overjoyed; we didn't think we were going to get paid!

The 'Burns Olympic 4' with Roy Green on the left. Roy's mother made our band waistcoats!

GOING WILD

'The silent sow sucketh the most swill'
Bob Cole – Horticulturalist

During one of our chats in the shop when there were no customers to be served, My friend Roy explained how much fun his job on the council was. A lot of the work was outside in the open and there was lots of variation in the type of jobs that had to be done and the fun that was to be had. The money was also better and there was sick pay if you took time off. As well as that, there was time and a half for working Saturdays and double time for working Sundays. It sounded good and so I decided once more to change my job. The staff at Saville's were all married and quite a lot older than me and I wanted the company of younger people to work with. I applied for a job at the nursery where my friend Roy was working, and got the job with a view to starting an apprenticeship in horticulture in due course.

Working at the nursery was so much fun with hose fights, clod fights, pot fights, smoke bombs and loads of other highly dangerous pursuits and games that took place when we should all have been working. I discovered the joys of conversation when 5 or 6 of us had to sit in a circle for days taking Geranium cuttings. Usually three of us younger ones and three older ones were assigned to the job. There was nothing to do whilst sitting facing each other, but talk. The conversations were animated and often argumentative, and I would listen carefully to all of the points of view, amazed at the amount of knowledge and wisdom that sprang forth. I learnt about girls (of course we were all male workers), sex, travel, foreign countries, war, Hitler, Unions, immigration, suicide and loads of other topical subjects that I knew nothing about. These conversations were often started by the older ones, whilst us younger lads joined in with giggling, rapport, comments and questions designed to ignite or inflame the discussion.

Working in the nursery at Enfield 1961

During the Summer months we would have our lunch down by the swimming pool which was just a couple of minutes walk from the nurseries and situated at the edge of Enfield Playing fields. The pool was a large open air 'lido' (now Southbury Leisure Centre), and as most of the staff from the nursery enjoyed swimming, we would have our sandwiches and then everyone would be having fun in the pool. Everyone that is, except me. I don't know where it came from but I have always had a strong fear of water.

Years earlier, whilst in junior school, we had to walk to the same pool once a week for swimming lessons. I hated these lessons and did everything I could to get out of taking part. We had to sit on the edge of the pool, jump in and swim a few feet on our own. I could not do this and shook with fear at the thought of jumping into the water. Eventually the teacher pushed me in. I think I got a small white stripe sewn onto my swimming trunks for 'jumping' in.

At lunchtimes, when we went from the nursery to the pool, I always donned my swimming trunks but of course could never swim like the others. My nursery friends did try to teach me; one holding my legs and one holding my head whilst I was on my back horizontal in the water. I know now that this was the worst possible way to try to teach anyone to swim and eventually they gave up and left me in peace at the side of the pool. One poor child drowned in the pool at about this time, and this morbidly gave me justification for not getting in the water and not getting wet. As a toddler, I even hated having my face washed with water. In later years I decided to face this fear and do something about it. You cant go through your whole life being fearful of something - anything.

As well as Roy and myself, there was one other young person working at the nursery; Richard Stockley. Richard became a lifelong friend, one whose humour and craziness reached ever new heights and whose comments in these 'Geranium days' drove the older members into fits of total frustration, anger or despair. The three of us got on really well. Roy was quite an intellect, Richard was a crazy 'tongue in cheek' kind of person, always the devils advocate, and I was liberating myself from the shackles of shyness that had for so long affected my interaction with other people and the rest of the world.

The craziness at the nursery would start in quite a small way; one of us would walk past the potting shed and a clay pot would fly out and hit you rather painfully on the arm or the leg. There would be retaliation and more pots would be thrown against a background of manic laughter and shouting. One day I was in the potting shed and lobbed a pot at Richard. It was a bulls-eye - hit him right on the head! I silently closed the potting shed door whilst he recovered, but knowing where the pot came from he took immediate revenge. He grabbed one of the large heavy wheelbarrows that were always lined up for use, and started charging at the potting shed. I opened the door so that I could to try to deflect his attack and he charged even faster at me. I jumped back into the potting shed and slammed the door shut. CRUNCH! The wheelbarrow took the door right off of its hinges, across the potting shed, and straight into my arms! We were both in fits of laughter at the site of the door on the wrong side of the shed and the wheelbarrow parked upside down in the middle of the shed. At that point the foreman appeared with a look of total shock on his face. He was speechless with anger but eventually said 'What the bloody hell is going on?' 'The door just came off in my hands' was the only excuse I could think of. We couldn't hide the giggles and we both got punished by having to spend a whole day shredding and sterilising. (shovelling soil into a shredder all day and then sterilising it with a steam machine to prepare it for potting). Shredding and sterilising was one of the most hated jobs at the nursery. It basically involved shovelling soil continuously into a mechanical shredder and then shovelling it again into a steam machine which killed off any pests or unwanted seeds in the soil. This part of the job created an awful smell which could not be avoided and we had to continue doing it for the whole day! 'Get shredding and sterilising' were not words that you wanted to hear.

Sometimes the greenhouses had to be cleared of pests and vermin. To do this nicotine smoke bombs were positioned inside and all around the greenhouse and then set alight - the furthest away from the door first. Of course, if word got out that this was being done, a couple of us would hide outside and hold the greenhouse door shut while the occupant choked himself silly, unable to escape the smoke that was meant to kill everything except the plants! Naturally the door was opened kindly just before death occurred, but when the door was finally opened the occupant just fell spluttering and coughing onto the floor outside. The nicotine 'bombs' have subsequently been banned from use in the UK.

You had to always be careful of water attacks outside during the Summer. Someone who was watering the frames full of thirsty plants would hide and drench you with the hose if you came within range. If both of you had hoses then the fun would really start. I always wore just a pair of shorts when watering outside as it was inevitable that there would be a good soaking, together with a lot of laughter and shouting.

George Kemish - rest his soul - was the foreman, and looking back it seems that he did take a lot of 'stick' from all of us. He was not really cut out to be a boss; he was skilled and very knowledgeable about photography, horticulture and botany but couldn't really keep the workforce disciplined. He would seem to talk to the plants and treat them as if they were people. He was a depressive and often talked about suicide and death. This together with his homosexuality made him a target for all of our cruel jokes and pranks.

One prank that went very wrong happened during one very hot Summer when we had to whitewash the outside of the greenhouse glass to stop the sun burning the plants inside. A very large cauldron on wheels, full of whitewash would be pumped by two people. The whitewash would be pumped at great pressure into a hose for the sprayer, who would walk along the gullies formed by the roofs of the long greenhouses, in order to spray everything white. The gully was only a few inches wide with the glass roofs of the greenhouses on the right and left. The cauldron had two large handles - one each side - so that two people could pump the whitewash by pushing backwards and forwards with the handles. Pumping the handles built up a pressure in the hose so that you could pump for a few minutes and then have a rest whilst the pressure in the hose lowered by the spraying. George, the foreman, was the 'sprayer' on this particular day on top of the greenhouses, and he would shout out for more pumping if the pressure dropped, or shout out stop if the pressure had built up enough to spray a good area of glass. Richard and I were the 'pumpers' and George called out for us to stop pumping as he had enough pressure in the hose to spray. We looked at each other with winks and smiles and carried on pumping. George called out again, louder

"Right, you can stop pumping now."

We carried on pumping even harder, the pressure

building up more and more.

"Stop bloody pumping NOW."

Then, CRASH. There was a scream and an almighty crash of broken glass. The hose had exploded spraying George with whitewash and sending him crashing through the greenhouse roof and onto the floor below! He emerged from the greenhouse covered in whitewash and blood, livid. We had to force ourselves not to burst out laughing.

"We didn't hear you shout stop" - we both managed to say in unison, and then escaped around the corner to roll on the floor in fits of laughter.

I developed quite an interest in horticulture and particularly botany, passing my RHS exam whilst studying at Chelsea Physics Garden during evenings. I enjoyed learning about genetics, DNA and chromosomes, and picked up the Latin terminology used for the naming of all plants quite naturally. I formed a special interest in cacti and succulents and was given a large section of a greenhouse in the nursery to propagate and grow these interesting plants. Amidst all of the fun and practical jokes that continued on a daily basis at work, I also managed to pass the City and Guilds exam in horticulture.

Still not sure if this was the right direction to take, I signed up for an apprenticeship in horticulture with the local council. Three years, with action on the tree gang, in the parks and playing fields, and of course in the nursery. Day release courses and visits to other horticultural establishments such as Wisley, and Kew were also part of the perks, but I didn't really feel that this was my chosen career; I still wanted to become successful with music and my guitar.

I introduced my own brand of 'nursery humour'

around the various local parks and on the tree gang, none of which was very well appreciated by the ageing staff of park keepers and tree pruners. I was getting itchy feet again, and then a golden opportunity appeared; ESCA (Enfield Sports and Cultural Association), were short of two people for their forthcoming sport and cultural exchange trip to Gladbeck in Germany. I had never been abroad before and relished the opportunity of travelling. My friend Richard Stockley joined ESCA as a table tennis player and I joined the cultural section on the strength of my music and the fact that I could play a couple of tunes on the guitar. Things were about to go into orbit, but more about that a little later on.

These days working at the nursery were wild. As well as the terrible acts of mischief that took place during working hours, there was a lot of fun to be had during evenings and particularly at weekends. Richard Stockley had a large circle of friends - a group of tearaways, and of course I was included in and became part of this gang, one of whom was an old childhood friend of mine from my early years at Bush Hill Park junior school; Ron Taylor. The nucleus of the gang Ron, together with Twiggy - (David Ridley), Richard, myself and a couple of others, created a formidable gang whose main purpose was to have fun.

Ron was the natural leader as he had the car. He was cool, efficient and reliable and generally what he said went. Our natural exuberance was tempered by Ron's cool headed attitude, and although he enjoyed all of our antics, he viewed them in much the same way as a parent might enjoy seeing his children playing or making mischief.

I am ashamed to say we terrorised country villages and towns during weekends when we travelled out to the country - even as far as Wales, a car load of noisy, leery youths, well-oiled with cans of beer and ready to frighten local pensioners and village cops with our noisy anarchy and totally uncontrolled behaviour. Our agenda was not to rob, harm or maim, but to have fun in the most daring and unpredictable way possible.

We took pillows and sleeping bags with us and slept rough anywhere we could find; a barn, a shed, or a derelict building would suffice, giving us just a few hours of sleep before the next day's adventures. Whilst driving through Aberystwyth, we thought it might be an entertaining idea to empty the feathers out of one of our pillows that had started to leak its contents. The shock on the faces of the locals seeing clouds of white feathers flying from a car speeding along the high street in this sleepy little town, provided us with the incentive to do the same to ALL of our pillows, and within a minute or two the high street and it's inhabitants were covered in feathers which flew in all directions - the contents of six sweaty pillows.

Groups of young girls were chatted up (mainly by Richard who was very good at this), and although most of them were wary of us, some were friendly and succumbed to the charms of Richard (and the much lesser intoxicated charms of the rest of us), exchanging kisses and cuddles.

Local 'bobbies' were at a loss to know how to deal with this rowdy group of youths which gained in confidence and daring as the hours went by. One poor copper ended up having his bike thrown over a bridge and into a river after he tried to reprimand us for breaking into a farmhouse which seemed to be uninhabited (but wasn't). Local police did not have the luxury of cars to swan around in, but mainly relied on bikes to get them to the scene of any crime or local disturbance, and a whistle to announce the presence of the law. I am not proud of any of this now, but it is history, it did happen, and so it is included.

Local beachside concerts and shows were disrupted and spoiled as we took to open stages, uninvited, in a drunken state, dancing or singing in a completely inappropriate manner. Visits to seaside resorts were always a challenge for our daring and our silliness. Our actions were nothing short of anarchy but after a couple of days of this craziness, we always returned home to catch up on sorely missed sleep.

THE POLICE

'Manners maketh the Man' – My Mum

My first experience of the Police in Enfield was with 'Copper Kirby', a constable who used to walk the streets of Enfield with his Police dog - a vicious and large Alsatian. If an offence was suspected - gathering in a group on the pavement, or making a nuisance of some kind, the dog would be let loose to apprehend the perpetrator of the 'crime', often not just apprehending but biting into the leg of the target. Copper Kirby was feared by the youth of Enfield during the years that he walked the streets of 'The Town'. We rode bikes around The Town, but at night the bikes had to have working front and rear lights. It was an offence to ride without these lights and if caught breaking the law, you would be in for a long night spent at Enfield Police station (then at the junction of London Rd and Genotin Rd). You had to watch carefully at the traffic lights where all cars and bikes would stop for a red light, and If you succumbed to the temptation to 'jump' the lights and cycle across when a red light was showing, Copper Kirby's dog would be after you snapping at your legs as you were peddling as fast as possible into the night. I must confess that I was chased by Copper Kirby and his dog on one or two occasions.

The traffic lights at road junctions could quite easily be manipulated by a cyclist. On approach to the lights there would be a rubber traffic sensor set in the tarmac across the road. After a certain amount of traffic had passed over the rubber strip, the lights would change from red to green. If a cyclist rode over the strip and suddenly applied brakes accurately at the top of the rubber strip, the force would bear down onto the sensor and the traffic lights would change conveniently to green, so that there would be no waiting around for the lights to change.

Public telephone boxes could also be used to make 'free' telephone calls. The number required would have to be 'tapped' on the hook of the telephone with a certain amount of taps for each digit of the phone number; five taps for the number five, eight taps for number eight, and so on. The letters for the telephone number (all telephone numbers had a three digit exchange code such as ENF for Enfield), were tapped in with a representative amount of taps for each particular letter. It would take a minute or two to skilfully complete the taps and get connected, but it was worth it, we had a free telephone call for as long as was required. We considered that we were beating the law when these minuscule legal aberrations were made, but the law and the Police always won the game.

The Police were feared in those days, and for that reason, on November 5th, we were all careful to stay clear of any Police who were on duty. There were more police than usual for Guy Fawkes night, especially around Chase Side and the Chase Green area of Enfield where there was always a large bonfire and plenty of fireworks. My friends and I had been to another bonfire party, and at 10.00 p.m.

after things had died down, we decided to visit Chase Green to see if there was any further fun to be had. We walked happily four abreast down Church St towards Chase Green, and on the way there we saw four Police Constables heading towards us, in fact they were heading straight for us. It would have been foolish to have maintained our 'formation' and so we split - two to the left and two to the right, so that the Police could continue on their journey without interruption. I was walking in the road and my friend John Garbutt was walking on the edge of the kerb, but as the police reached us, one of them elbowed John into the road. The policemen stopped and told John to watch where he was walking. I got angry and shouted that I saw him being pushed into the road.

"Right, you can come with us."

Our other two friends disappeared and the Police tried to capture John and myself. A Police car arrived, and John protesting, was bundled in. I was then captured from behind by one of the Policemen and I rammed my elbow into his stomach to escape, running away down the centre of Church St. Another Police car lights flashing and siren blaring pulled up and more Police arrived. I was being chased by eight or more Policemen, and eventually I was captured and pushed into the back of the second Police car. I quickly saw my chance, opening the door and leaping out of the opposite side of the car and into the road. The chase began again, but it was not long before I was caught and more securely dumped in the rear of the car, this time with a Policeman sitting each side holding me in. I was threatened with a piece of lead piping;

"Make a fuss and you'll get this"

and within seconds I was being marched into the tradesman's entrance at the rear of Enfield Police Station.

John was already there with quite a few other detainees of all ages - some sober, some drunk, some angry and some just upset. One poor old man was blind drunk and dropped all of the contents of his pockets on the floor after demands were made for him to empty his pockets. He was on his knees with his head being rammed into the handkerchief, squashed cigarette packet and the few coins that were his possessions, by an angry Sergeant demanding that he pick the items up. I gave a false name and address when I was questioned and was consequently thrown into a cell until my real details could be confirmed. John was charged with 'insulting behaviour' and was soon collected by his angry Father. I was later also charged with 'insulting behaviour' and was eventually freed the following morning.

The four of us met up the next day, angry at our unjust experiences with the local Police. John's Father, a quite well off pharmacist, vowed to get us legal representation at court which he did, and after being pronounced guilty and both being fined £75, he became even more angry and threatened to take the case to the appeal court in London. True to his word he did this and we all arrived in Parliament Square dressed in our 'Sunday Best' for the hearing at the appeal court. "Case dismissed!" shouted the judge. I did not even know what the words meant and had to ask John's disappointed Father what was going on. He was even more upset than I was at the verdict - well I suppose he must have been, he had paid a lot to get the case to the appeal court and had to pay the court costs and John's £75.00 fine as well. Sometimes you win, sometimes you lose; this time we lost.

In retrospect, it may have been easier to have spoken to the Police at the beginning and said; "You must know my Father, Sergeant Stockley, 'Y' Division, Tottenham." This was a line used by my friend Richard whenever we were apprehended by the Police. It always worked and we were always let off. Richard's Dad really was a copper at Tottenham but I don't think he ever knew how many times his name had been used as a means of escape. Later on, when we had cars, Richard used to leave a copy of the Police Journal on the front dashboard, this always ensured that no penalties would be issued by the Police for minor traffic infringements. Clever, huh?

If you were young in those days, the Police were never far away; always ready to warn, threaten or intimidate you in some way. At least we knew limits; things you could get away with and things you couldn't get away with, although it felt great on the few occasions when we did get away with the odd misdemeanour.

NEW HORIZONS

'Logical sequential deduction'
Charles Traynor, Langham Radio

I was 17. I had passed my driving test (on the third attempt), and now wanted a car. I put the word about that I was looking for a cheap car, and sure enough, after just a couple of days, I got a result. A friend of a friend was selling a 1937 Austin 7 'Ruby' for £20.00. I dragged a couple of mates along who sounded like they knew a bit about cars, and we found the Austin 7 parked in the road by its owner. I tried to appear mechanical and got under the car, I kicked the wheels and tapped the bodywork a little. I suggested that there was some rust, and that one of the tyres looked rather worn. I offered £10.00 (which was all I had). The offer was accepted and I drove my friends home in my first ever car – (untaxed and uninsured).

Quite often the car would be packed with various friends, and friends of friends. There was actually a sun roof which slid back and enabled the occupants to stand up in the car shouting out to passers by and generally making a nuisance of themselves. The car had 'character.' There was also a sun windscreen, which could be partially opened to let the breeze flow through the car. Another friend - Peter Pye (who was also a guitar player) suggested that the car, which was plain black, would look good re-painted. He ran a signwriting business with his father and had access to good quality paints and varnishes. I decided that the colour should be canary yellow and British Racing Green, and plans were made to strip the paint from the car and begin painting. The job had to be done in short bursts when the signwriting business was quiet, and so for a couple of weeks I was driving around in a silver bodied car that had been stripped down to the bare metal bodywork. The two front doors were also missing as they were being painted separately, and so the whole operation of driving was really quite hazardous - but a lot of fun.

My first car after it had been painted by Peter Pye and his Dad, Frank Pye.
With Vic Long, Dave Morgan and myself on the right.

Eventually the painting was finished; a coat of primer, then an undercoat, and two top coats, finished with a wonderful glossy layer of varnish. It looked superb in bright yellow and green and drew the attention of everyone including naturally, the local police. Of course once the police knew that the car was roadworthy, taxed and insured, they did not cause too many problems and seemed to discontinue their regular inspections of engine, chassis and documents. I was, however, chased by a police car as I drove from Oakwood Station downhill towards Enfield Town. I discovered that the car in spite of its age, could do more than seventy miles per hour in top gear, and I certainly enjoyed being chased by the police car which seemed to have difficulty in keeping up with my old Austin 7. The chase eventually came to an end and I was stopped at 'The Triangle' in Palmers Green where the police lifted the bonnet of the car expecting to find an aircraft engine or at least an illegal racing engine of gigantic proportions. There were looks of disbelief as they looked at the old rusty Austin 7 engine and I was let off with a 'caution,' probably because no one in a court of law would actually believe that a car of this age would actually be capable of doing seventy miles per hour.

The life of the car would be brought to a sudden halt however. Whilst driving down Wellington Road towards Enfield, a car shot out of a side turning and smashed into the offside of my car. I could not get out and had to climb over to the passenger side of the car to escape. A very old man had driven into me and he explained that he didn't see my car! I grabbed him by the lapels, screamed at him

"How can you *not* see a bright yellow and green car? You silly old bastard!"

I was almost crying with rage and felt awful explaining to Peter Pye that all of his beautiful work had been ruined.

The whole door and door post was so badly damaged that the car was beyond repair. It was still running well, but the only way I could continue to use the car was by getting in and out of the passenger side whilst receiving daily warnings from the police about driving my poor badly damaged car.

At this point in time I had made friends with two very attractive ladies - Beryl and her sister. Beryl was in her 30s, separated from her husband, and had three young children. With her and her children, the five of us had a great time zooming around in that battered old yellow car; the kids loved it and I enjoyed becoming a kind of surrogate father to them, as their real father had disappeared some time previously. I actually moved in with Beryl for a few months and had my first taste of what it was like to be a family man, at the age of twenty.

One evening I took Beryl, her sister and a few of her friends up to the West End in the car. We became quite tipsy after visiting quite a few bars and clubs. If there were any drinking and driving laws I did not know of them, there were certainly no seat belts in those days. I was showing off the speed of the car on the return journey, and as we reached the traffic lights at Finsbury Park, I braked hard as the traffic lights glowed red and the cars in front of me had come to a halt. The surprise was that nothing happened. The car did not show any sign of slowing down. The brakes had completely failed. There was nothing for it but to swerve over onto the opposite side of the road in order to miss the stationary cars that were waiting for the lights to change. I swerved and drove onto the other side of the road as the lights changed to green and the oncoming traffic started moving in my direction. I could not get back onto my own side of the road as the traffic had now started to move forward and so took a chance to drive between both lines of moving traffic. I hit a BMW coming towards me and heard the scrape of metal gouging the side of both cars. There was nothing to do but put my foot down and 'legit', but looking in the rear view mirror I could see that the BMW driver had turned his car around and was weaving in and out of the traffic in order to catch me up. The girls were screaming and laughing. The sun roof was open and one or two of our group were standing up giving a progress report about the speed and position of the car that was now chasing us. I could also hear Police car sirens and see a police car in the rear view mirror as the BMW overtook me on the wrong side of the road and pushed my car into the kerb. At this point the police also arrived but to my surprise instead of arresting me for dangerous driving, they took the driver of the BMW and pinned him down on the bonnet of his own car. We were asked to get out to give a statement of what had happened. The girls laid it on, stating that this lunatic had been following us and swerved in front of us after driving on the wrong side of the road, and damaging (yes, you've guessed it), the off side drivers door and door post. We were all allowed to continue on our journey, but the driver of the BMW was taken away protesting loudly in a Police car. The following day one of the coppers arrived at Beryl's house under the pretext of making further investigations, and asked her out for a date. She took his telephone number and promised to give him a ring to arrange something. We never heard from the police about that incident and of course Beryl never made that telephone call.

After a couple more warnings from the police that they would have to prosecute me for the unroadworthy condition of the vehicle, I had to get rid of my dear old Austin 7. I did not want to look at the scrap dealer whilst he towed the car away. I got the full market value of the car from the insurance company - £10 - the amount I paid for the car and which was included on my original insurance proposal. That little car and the memories of it meant a lot to me.

The time arrived for the trip to Gladbeck in Germany with ESCA. There were around forty of us going on the trip, and we were all billeted to host families upon our arrival in Germany. On arrival in Gladbeck we were taken to a large hall where the host families were lined up facing us. As each of our names were called out, we had to step forward to meet our hosts. I was one of the last names to be called and saw a giant of a man whose family was to be my host for the duration of the trip. Most of the host families were involved with sport in some way, and my host, Detlev Rothenstein, was a champion discus thrower. I was becoming somewhat concerned that I could not live up to anyone's expectations in music or indeed in sport. Detlev did not say much, he was quite formal and stern looking, but we drove back to his parents' apartment in his 'Aronde' sports car the speed of which which took my mind away from the immediate problem of representing ESCA and Enfield.

On the second evening of our stay, we had some free time and Detlev decided to take me out for some beer so that we could get to know each other. The beer was served in litre mugs and I sampled quite a few of the various local beers available. We had food too - some bierwirst (a kind a sausage) and then more beer. At the end of the evening we found ourselves back at Detlev's home. His Mother had left us a strawberry gâteaux on the table for supper.

"Come! We must eat!" said Detlev.

Not wanting to offend, I ate and ate, in fact we both finished off the strawberry gâteaux whilst laughing and joking in an alcohol induced kaleidoscope of odd English and German words using our very limited bi-lingual vocabulary. I had my own small bedroom and immediately upon lying down, the nausea hit me. There was not enough time to get up and get to the toilet. I decorated the room, the walls, the quilt and the curtains with the most awful pink coloured, strawberry smelling vomit! I must have made a lot of noise as within seconds, Detlev and his mother Frau Rothenstein were in the room. Detlev's mother was screaming at him - probably blaming him for my condition. I cannot describe the embarrassment of standing naked in a stranger's home after decorating the room with my awful smelling vomit. I spent the whole of the next day apologising to Mr and Mrs Rothenstein, grovelling and trying as hard as possible to be on my very best behaviour. I discovered that Mr Rothenstein was in the SS during the second world war, and a day or two after the 'Gâteaux incident' he proudly showed me his photo collection, illustrating him and his colleagues in full Nazi uniform. I took this as a warning not to get drunk and mess the room up again.

Richard was billeted in a house *full* of people! Mr and Mrs Mittlestadt had two daughters, a cousin and two lads around our age with them in their home. All of the host families shared social drinks and meals with us visitors, and I particularly enjoyed going to Richard's family as their cousin, Sabine Kussmaul, was the most beautiful girl I had ever seen. Kussmaul translated means kissmouth which seemed to make her even more alluring. I couldn't take my eyes off of her whenever we were all together, and in the garden she would sit on my lap to talk or joke or listen to me trying to strum my guitar. If we went out in the Mittlestadts' car she would be on my lap again squashed in the back and giggling away. I had never had these feelings before and fell madly in love with her (well, teenagers' love anyway).

The hormones in me were going wild, and tongue in cheek, I blame this on my education, more precisely Tottenham Tech, and even more precisely, Fred Shelley the art teacher. Fred, as he was affectionately known, was a popular teacher; all of the lads loved him. He had personality and a rather suave Alan Ladd kind of appearance. His white slicked back hair must have been blond in years gone by, and although a great teacher, there was something sad about him; a failed relationship, a missed opportunity, or just something missing from his life. To our great pleasure, he often referred to the female form as a gift of art from God. He even had scantily clothed maidens - pictures from magazines - pinned to the art room wall. He would describe the smooth roundness of the tummy or the firm strong thigh supporting the wonderful curves of the upper torso. We stood dribbling, looking at these pictures, listening unblinking to Fred's detailed descriptions. Art was probably the most popular lesson in the college, and we would stand watching the pictures and listening to Fred with embarrassing bulges appearing in the front our trousers! How could you not like a lesson like that? We all got good marks in Fred's lessons. Hence my eternal appreciation of the female form!

My feelings for Sabine however, were unfortunately never physically manifest, but even though there was a language problem, we always seemed to be giggling and having fun together. There was, to my extreme disappointment, never ever more than a kiss on the cheek, which actually seemed to intensify my amorous feelings for her even further.

Various trips and outings were arranged for the free time that was available. On one such occasion, we went deep underground into the coal mine which formed part of Gladbeck's industrial history. There were also parties and plenty of sporting events, most of which we skipped. Richard and me had a great time with the two lads from his host family, Gotz and Jorg, drinking beer and doing the crazy things that teenage boys tend to do. We did not want the trip - the party, or the friendships - to end, and when it came time to leave and get on the coach traveling back to England, Richard and I made a pact not to go back home!

Everyone on the coach thought we were joking as we waved goodbye to them. There was a warning for us to get onto the coach, then a second warning and then a very serious third. The coach started moving; we were not on it. We waved it out of sight and cheered ourselves and our bravery. We had previously spoken to our hosts - the Rothensteins and the Mittlestadts, about the possibility of staying on with them for a couple more weeks and getting work to help pay for our keep. There was guarded and rather apprehensive agreement to this, and so we felt obliged to look for work in Gladbeck as quickly as possible.

We found work for a large garden landscaping company, and had to be picked up by bus early every morning and taken to the various sites to do our work. Instead of tea breaks, there were 'beer breaks' with one of the older members of the team cycling to the shops to get the beer for all of us. The beer had to be cold, as the work was hard and the weather was hot. I guess we were paying for our sins doing this laborious work with the Summer sun beating down on our backs. Richard and I didn't always work on the same job, and so we nearly always met up in the evenings to exchange information about the day's work and events that coloured the experience of working in Germany.

A telegram from Enfield Council soon arrived. I was to return immediately, or my apprenticeship would be terminated and my job relinquished. Richard had a similar communication. We decided to stay. The fun we were having was more important than our jobs back home. The work in Germany was going well, apart from the fact that a few of the very old workers who, in the truck on the way to work, seemed intent on blaming me personally for damage caused by the bombing raids of World War 2. "Du bist ein dumnkopf" was one of the first phrases that I learnt and I used this to inflame the German/English post war relationship even further, in fact I was expecting World War 3 to erupt as a result of some rather heated exchanges between myself and some of these bitter old German workers.

We continued working in Germany for a further few months, but eventually it became time to return to England. I vowed to return and suggested to Sabine that one day I may arrive at her home in Northern Germany.

The bond between myself and Richard became extremely strong as we both looked after each other's interests and welfare during our time in Germany and the time we spent hitching back to England by car, boat and train.

The job had gone, I had lost my car, and I had

no money or savings. Desperate times require desperate measures; I had to have a car and some money. Fortune smiled and I interviewed for a job, with a car as part of the job package. Langham Radio (now gone) based at Bush Hill Parade, was looking for an electrical repair man who could collect and deliver electrical items from customers, repair them on site or bring them back to the shop to repair.

"Of course I can repair electrical items", came my rehearsed reply at the onset of the interview. (I must have had more front than Harrods). I was offered the job with a one month probationary period and the condition that I looked after the car during the evenings and weekends as it could not be left in the road unattended during these times. Great! I was mobile again and now I could concentrate on my own priorities; getting enough money together to get back to Germany, and getting the guitar, music and a group going properly.

The rock group craze had really taken off in the local areas of Enfield, Edmonton, Waltham Cross and Cheshunt. Cliff Richard from Cheshunt had become a National superstar. Buster Meikle and the Day Breakers (Russ Ballard on guitar), from Waltham Cross, were now doing big tours. Big names came to Waltham Cross each week and played at the 'Imp' - (The Imperial Hall, still there and now resurrected as the Waltham Cross Conservative Club). B Bumble and the Stingers, Johnny Kidd and the Pirates, Bruce Channel, Screaming Lord Sutch, Joe Brown, Neil Christian and the Crusaders (Jimmy Page on guitar!) and many other big 'names' of the time, regularly played at the 'Imp' and so if you were not playing somewhere yourself, you would be at the Imp with loads of other musicians and young people. I had improved as a guitarist somewhat and played with various local groups. I turned down an offer to join a band that was to tour Norway and Sweden as I was intent on returning to Germany with some money in my pocket. The group returned to England after their tour, changed its name to Procul Harum and had a number one hit record! Sometimes you make the wrong decision.

I was asked to join a local band with a big following, the only problem was they wanted a bass player and not a guitarist. They had loads of gigs lined up and a manager who ensured that they played locally most evenings and weekends. I took the job and together with my day job, managed to accumulate some money and some 'on the road' experience using a bass guitar borrowed from a friend. I was now a member of 'The Deep Blues' (the name was eventually changed to 'The Moquette') and we played lots of the local rock pubs and clubs. The band was really ahead of its time and, prior to the Who, was smashing up equipment and using feedback as part of the show. The music was anarchy, like a 1960s version of Punk rock. You either liked or hated The Deep Blues!

'The Deep Blues' - *later on known as 'The Moquette'*

The manager of Langham Radio was a gentleman named Charlie Trayhorn, a clever, inspirational and remarkable man who was becoming increasingly concerned about my bleary eyed and disheveled appearance every morning caused by late nights playing in the band. It was also obvious that I could only repair the very basic electrical appliances such as toasters or hair dryers. TVs were totally out of the question. To Charlie's credit he offered me the job after my one month was up. I liked him and I think he saw me as a wayward son that he had to straighten out and educate. His intelligence was superb, and he taught me to fix electrical appliances using the three words **logical, sequential, deduction**, a way of tracing the fault from the point where the electrical input enters the appliance to the point where the problem occurs. I still remember his words and the wonderful conversations we enjoyed, as we worked together in the electrical workshop.

Charlie introduced me to the fascination of the Martial Arts in a strange omen and precursor of the direction my life would take years later. Himself a successful fencer, he would describe in great detail the concentration, the Martial spirit, and the tactics that he would use against an opponent whilst fencing, or how minute movements of the little finger controlled the rapier and his opponent. He was a fascinating man, and six months later I was to completely disregard all of the help and kindness he had given me. I regret that moment and regret not showing my appreciation of him in a better way.

The Deep Blues were getting more and more popular and we were playing now at packed venues almost every night. The manager announced that he had secured a tour of England and Wales for us and I felt the problems of loyalty stirring deep inside me. The tour would be at least one month long, playing in all of the major UK cities and towns. None of the other members of the group had jobs and so they were free to go on the tour. I was working and had to decide either to quit the band and carry on with my job or do the tour and say goodbye to the job. I knew that Charlie would not be able to manage for a month without any help. I spent many lonely hours pondering all of the consequences of this situation and knew that I had to do the tour.

I could not bring myself to tell Charlie. He always seemed to be helping me or explaining an interesting point to me. The days moved on and preparations were in an advanced stage for the tour. I had to tell Charlie I was going to leave, and after work on the Saturday before the tour began, I locked the car for the last time and took a bus to Charlie's house in Enfield Town. I stood tongue tied on the doorstep and he stood facing me in surprise.

"I've got to leave the job" I blurted out. I explained that the band had a tour lined up.

"When have you got to leave?"

"Now Charlie, I'm really sorry."

That was the last time I saw Charlie. I was as upset as he was.

I will never know if my decision was a mistake or not, but I felt terrible guilt about letting Charlie down in this way. He was like a kind of Father to me. The tour went ahead and was fraught with transport and accommodation problems. It seemed as though most of the time we were sleeping in the van with the equipment, and going into a public toilet in the mornings to get washed and cleaned up. The venues where we were playing were often pretty awful and one night after a particularly bad gig we came out to find that the four tyres on our van had been slashed. I did get experience of playing to big crowds though, and after the tour felt as though I could do anything or play anywhere. During that month you could say we paid our dues.

Letters were exchanged regularly between Sabine in Germany and myself here in England. Her letters were very artistic, often decorated with beautiful borders on the pages of the letters, and sometimes on the envelopes themselves. Sometimes a sketch or picture would also be enclosed, and I would try to gauge from all of this artwork the state of her mind and if she had strong feelings for me. Of course the letters were all written in German - a lovely script that only Europeans seem to use. One very large letter arrived with its envelope covered in small denomination stamps. I had to beg a supply of halfpenny orange stamps from the post office and do the same in return, covering a large A4 envelope in bright orange stamps.

I arranged with Sabine to travel over to her home in Germany by car (although I didn't actually have a car) in the new year. Letters were exchanged and I introduced my friend Johnny Garbutt to Sabine's sister Suzi and they both started writing letters to each other as well. I saved hard and accumulated £100, enough to buy a second hand Hillman Husky that I had seen for sale.

I purchased the car and suggested to Johnny that it would be good for him to also be on the trip so that he could have the chance to meet Suzi. It was February and I was itching to go. Everyone suggested leaving the trip until the Winter was over and weather improved, but the journey was planned, I was excited, and Frau Kussmaul had agreed that we could stay in a spare room in their house.

The AA sent me a detailed road plan of our journey to Wahlstedt bei Segeberg in Northern Germany, taking us through France, Holland and Belgium. We began the trip singing as we drove, looking forward to seeing our two German 'girlfriends'. We were in great spirits and slept in the car whilst in France to save money paying for hotel accommodation. The car although old, seemed to be running quite well. We didn't rush but stopped quite often for food, drinks and petrol. Unfortunately, whilst we were driving through Belgium, the car decided to break down - steam pouring from the radiator. We called the AA in Belgium and the mechanic informed us that the radiator had a bad leak and was unserviceable. Big problems such as this were not part of our plan, especially as the Hillman Husky was an old model and parts such as a radiator were extremely difficult to locate.

The AA could only offer to locate a suitable radiator in England and have it shipped over. This would take days, probably weeks, and we decided to look for a car scrap yard locally, and perhaps find a similar sized radiator that may fit the car. We found a breakers yard on the outskirts of a small Belgian town. We slowly drove in, radiator steaming, and found the owner, asking him if he may have a radiator that could possibly fit our car. This request seemed to create some considerable excitement and he ran dragging us along with him to the corner of the yard pointing to a large pile of dumped broken cars. There at the top of the pile was a Hillman Husky, the same year and the same colour as my own. It was a chance in a million. These cars were never the most popular of cars and to find one like this in Belgium was nothing short of miraculous. Within an hour the radiator was taken out and fitted to our car. We were back in business and on route to our destination.

As we drove further North through Germany the weather turned bad. Strong winds and snow made driving difficult. We were traveling at night on the autobahn route towards Hamburg, the snow seemed to get thicker and thicker, very strong winds making conditions even worse. The snow was so intense that I had to slow down, the windscreen wipers were only just clearing the snow on the windscreen and I could barely see what was ahead. The front wheel of the car became stuck in a groove along the edge of the motorway, and as I turned the steering wheel to get out of the groove the car swerved sideways across the motorway. I tried to straighten the car up, we skidded as I instinctively braked. The car turned over and I remember seeing sparks as the bonnet scraped along the surface of the motorway. The car landed upside down in the fast lane of the autobahn, with cars screaming past us, swerving out of the way to avoid us and other cars that had piled into one another. I was now out of the car and waving my arms to try to slow down the oncoming traffic. It was no good; they were all traveling so fast it was impossible to brake with so much snow and ice everywhere. I looked for Johnny but he was not in the car. Yards ahead I saw a leg sticking out from underneath the central reservation, and I ran expecting to see the rest of him somewhere else detached from his leg. He had been thrown from the car and landed around 15 yards away. In the glare of car headlights he looked awful, and in desperation I lifted his head and slapped his face shouting "wake up, wake up." His eyes opened and I dragged him out from underneath the central reservation. Cars were still crashing and screeching past us, and then I must have passed out, as I remember nothing else but waking up in hospital the next day.

Johnny was in a bed next to me, and the rest of the ward was filled with injured drivers and passengers from the events of the previous night. We were getting angry looks from the other occupants of the beds, and so said nothing, hoping that they would not realise that I was the cause of their injuries.

We were inspected by the doctors and told that we must stay in hospital for observation. We were also told that our host family had been contacted and were on their way to see us. Three hours later the Kussmaul family entered the ward to see us in bed, bruised and covered in bandages. The joy of seeing them all was overtaken by the sheer embarrassment of causing the family so much stress and worry. I felt like a fool; the anticipation of a wonderful reunion with Sabine and her family was lost in the unhappy situation we found ourselves in.

Against all advice, we signed ourselves out of the hospital and travelled on to Wahlstedt with the Kussmaul family in their friends car. We had lost everything in the accident. My guitar, clothes and gifts for the family were all lost. We were of course made very welcome and had a pleasant time for the couple of weeks that had been planned. The cash we did have, was given to Frau Kussmaul to help with the cost of food for us. It was a time tinged with feelings of sadness that we had somehow spoilt forever the magic that may have been.

✳ ✳ ✳

We hitch hiked back to England feeling sorry for ourselves, with no car and no money. The letters from Sabine seemed less frequent and shorter in length. I had hoped that she might be able to come to England so that I could compensate in some small way for the upset I had caused her and her family. Eventually, the letters stopped altogether, and I was shocked that one year after our return, Frau Kussmaul wrote to me explaining that Sabine was pregnant. She was just 17 at that time. I was devastated, and received scorned looks from my Mother who considered that I must be to blame in some way for this predicament. We never had more than a few kisses, and it may well have been that Sabine already had her boyfriend whilst Johnny and I were over there. She sent me a picture of herself, happy, with her new baby daughter Katya and I hoped that the father managed to take care of them both. However, another big shock was on the way for me which took my mind away from the upset and sadness that I now felt.

The smashed up Hillman Husky that got us to Germany.

TRAUMA

**'Anything that doesn't totally destroy you,
only serves to make you stronger'
Terry Venables**

I t was now time for Summer holidays. A Farm
holiday in Gloucester was arranged, with
farm meals catered for and visits out to local places of
interest. The holiday didn't excite me, and apart from
that, I didn't feel like going away with my parents. I decided to stay at home, imagining the freedom that an
empty home can bring; friends around, parties, playing
my guitar as loud as I would like, records played until I
was too tired to stay awake. It was indeed like that for
a few days. Late nights and late mornings lying in, but
then my Uncle Hendy and Auntie Phil arrived one morning, looking very worried and concerned. There had been
a car accident while my Sister, Mum and Stepfather were
on holiday on the farm in Gloucester. While out for a
day trip driving to Wales there had been an accident
and judging by the appearance of my Uncle and Auntie,
a pretty serious one. They could not tell me any details,
but I rang the farmhouse and spoke to my Sister Jan who
was clearly upset. Thankfully she had at the last minute,
decided not to travel on the car journey to Wales but to
stay for the day at the farm.

I knew that I had to act and quickly arranged a bag to travel down to Gloucester. I took the train and arrived at Gloucester Station in the dark and at night. As I alighted from the train, I could see my Sister waiting alone at the far end of the dimly lit platform. She looked small, frail and lonely and her pale white face looked even more pale in the yellow lighting from the train platform. We cuddled for a moment and I tried to get more news of the events from her. Nothing was making any sense. Was she in the accident? What happened? where is Mum and Dad? Are they badly injured? We made our way to Gloucester Royal Infirmary and nothing in this world could have prepared me for what I saw. Mum was in a ward with other patients. She was covered in bandages and plaster. Her face was unrecognisable, bruised and blackened. Her eyes were not open. She was under heavy sedation and clearly it was miraculous that she had actually survived at all. I could see dozens of small cuts around her face and eyes where splintered glass had shattered her face. I was not prepared for this shock and felt the panic rising in me.

Our stepfather was in a small ward on his own. He did not look so badly injured as Mum. He made strange breathing noises through a hole which had been made in his throat. I learned that this was a tracheotomy to assist breathing as his lungs were damaged. He was in a coma, and although we spoke to him and even tried shouting, there was no sign that he had heard us, in fact there was no response at all just the steady wheezing of air passing in and out of the tracheotomy tube.

My mind was spinning, I couldn't make sense of anything and could not understand how this had happened as he was a very careful driver. I knew my Mum was in the passenger seat as she could not drive. The car was always kept in good shape and he never exceeded speed limits or jumped traffic lights. His driving advice to me was; "Be prepared for other people's mistakes", and so I found it difficult to see how a terrible accident like this had happened. We were told by the doctors that both parents were in very bad shape. The face of the doctor who explained this looked heavy with the burden of his duty. I felt as though my main task was to look after my sister Jan, and try to reassure her that everything would be ok. There was little else that could be done.

We arranged with the hospital to stay overnight in a small reception room until our parents recovered. We took it in turns to sleep on the couch and alternatively on the floor. Days passed and nights drew on while we slept each night in this little room. There was little change in either of our parents and in fact Mum probably looked worse, drifting in and out of consciousness with more facial bruising and swelling. Each day we continued to shout and talk to try to end the coma of our stepfather. It was strange but the only reaction from him was when the nurse touched or tickled his toe; the foot would retract just as a normal person might react to tickling. That was the only response there was. On the 11th day after the accident the doctors called us both into the corridor and told us that our stepfather had died. We went in to see him for the last time and he was in the same position as always; he never regained consciousness. We were consoled by the doctor's words that he would have been an invalid if he ever did recover; his brain was damaged by the limited supply of oxygen caused by the accident; his lungs were also badly damaged which caused problems with breathing.

What do we do? There are no informative leaflets from the council to advise on what action to take; no textbooks available with other people's advice taken from their experience of similar situations. We felt that we had to tell our Mum that her husband had died. This was difficult as she was not fully conscious or even fully aware of what had happened. She seemed to drift in and out of consciousness during that time. She had no recollection of the holiday or the accident and didn't understand where she in fact was. We decided that it would be best to not tell her, as the news may affect or impair her own recovery. I was 21 years old and arranging my stepfathers funeral. I contacted as many of his own family as possible, and one by one they all arrived at Gloucester for the funeral. We did feel it necessary to tell our Mum about the funeral, although she didn't understand and couldn't comprehend our words. Because of her injuries she could not talk and so the whole situation was really impossible to imagine. I also had to get involved with the solicitors who were dealing with the case. 'Letters of Administration' had to be invoked and the insurance company had to sue the driver of the coach, which had hit my stepfather's car head on whilst overtaking a tractor. It was a terrible situation, and we took our Mum home by train a couple of weeks later, one arm was still in plaster and the bruises and scars were still there. She didn't remember a thing about the accident or how it happened, but maybe that was for the best.

ROCK ON!

'To play great music cast your eyes upon a distant star'
Yehudi Menuin's Violin Teacher.

T hings were hotting up on the music front. I had helped to form a new band 'The Skylarks' with Peter Pye on rhythm guitar, Vic Long vocals, Chris Spooner on bass guitar and Barry Hebb on drums. We even had a manager, Dave Morgan, who was a local friend keen to see us progress. (Dave eventually became the Best Man at my first marriage and I at his.) Prior to us being called The Skylarks, we were known locally as 'The Bumblies.' We received a solicitor's letter threatening us with legal action if we continued using this name as there was a TV programme already with the same name. I can't imagine how a TV programme got to hear about us - The Bumblies - a very obscure local group of teenage lads unknown and trying to make it in the music business. Below is a picture of 'The Bumblies' before we were forced to change the name of the group to 'The Skylarks.'

It all sounds very innocent now, and it was, but we had a great time playing in the Church halls around the Enfield and Chingford areas.

'The Bumblies', later renamed as 'The Skylarks'.
Peter Pye, Barry Hebb, Chris Spooner and myself on the right.

The Skylarks played locally and had a pretty good set of rock and pop music. We had a good, albeit small, following of loyal friends and 'fans' who came along to support us wherever we were playing. Most of the 'gigs' were locally held and took place in various Church halls around the Enfield area on a Friday or Saturday evening. There was always a lot of excitement at these local events and usually a small amount of illicit alcohol would be consumed. When the show was over, the adrenalin would be pumping, and as any musician knows, it would be difficult to 'switch off'. At these times there would often be some fun to be had or pranks to join in with, and it was during one of these fun times that I foolishly ended up in Chase Farm Hospital.

Peter Pye had a large old Austin car at that time which carried most of us together with quite a bit of the equipment to and from the gigs. The car was full, and for some unknown reason I was lying down, legs apart on the roof of the car. Peter decided to drive off much to the amusement of everyone inside the car as well as myself laughing away on the roof. The car braked and I started sliding forward to the front of the car - down the windscreen and onto the bonnet. Those who remember the old Austin cars will know that the trademark metal emblem - a large flying 'A' with a symbolic wing attached to it, was situated at the front and in the middle of the bonnet and this is where the problem started. By the time the car had stopped I had slid forward and off of the bonnet onto the road with a terrible pain in my groin area. A crowd of friends surrounded me laughing and joking; I started laughing as well but shortly decided to go back home as I felt pretty awful. I was shocked at home when my Sister noticed that my jeans were soaking wet with blood. The flying 'A' had ripped through my jeans and into my lower region. Shocked, my trousers were taken off and the damage surveyed. There was so much blood it was difficult to see the actual damage and so I was bundled into a car and taken off to the local hospital. My jeans were unceremoniously ripped off and I was 'cleaned up' by a very large and scary Amazonian looking nurse. "Oh yes, you have a torn testicular sac" - and with that she produced a can of antiseptic spray, a needle and thread, deftly using her needlework skills to make good the damage to that very painful 'sac.' It was painful and of course very embarrassing, so be sure to think carefully before you lie on the roof of an Austin, (a Ford is probably OK though). The whole event provided a good source of entertainment for friends and fans for a long time after the pain had subsided.

The early 1960's was a great time for music. Rock n Roll was well established and The Beatles had had their first couple of big hit records. Any bands, singers or musicians from Liverpool had a distinct advantage over others from the South, as the 'Liverpool Sound', seen as a ticket to success, was being quickly picked up by managers, studios and record companies. Along with the Beatles, there was Gerry and the Pacemakers, Billy J Kramer, The Mersybeats, The Searchers and loads of others, all with the 'Liverpool sound'. The record companies were like sheep signing up any band or individual musician that came from Liverpool. Any music that came from Liverpool had a pedigree which was very well regarded by everyone in the music business and lapped up by the public in general.

I saw a great opportunity in a planned visit to Enfield by Liverpool's Brian Epstein, the manager of the Beatles and the man who got them their tours, records and success. I decided (naively) to try to meet him, after I discovered that he was to open a fete at the George Spicer School in Enfield. I considered that The Skylarks were so good that Mr Epstein would only have to hear us to sign us up with a record deal and propel us to stardom. I got the band and all of the equipment set up in the lounge at my home. Tuned up and ready to play, all I had to do was to get the Beatles manager into the room to see us and hear how good we were.

At the fete, I waited until the opening ceremony had finished and then approached Brian Epstein, politely introducing myself and inviting him to listen to our band. Without stopping for breath I included the offer of transport to my home - ready and waiting. He was bemused, smiling but more importantly, interested. I was excited and hopeful.

"I will have to speak to my transport manager, but yes, I would be happy to come and hear your band, The Skylarks."

I held my breath while the pair went into private conversation, whispering, with heads close together. Brian looking disappointed, turned to face me.

"I have to be at the London Palladium shortly for Cilla's (Cilla Black's) opening show there, unfortunately there won't be time to come and see your band. Please send me a tape of your music and I will be in touch." My face must have clearly registered my disappointment as he continued; "I'm really sorry."

So close but yet so far. I was sure that if he came to hear us play he would be excited by the music and offer us some kind of management. I returned home, tail between legs, explaining my efforts to the expectant band of musicians and knowing that we didn't have a tape to send Brian Epstein.

When we weren't playing ourselves, we used to go to the Mildmay Tavern in Balls Pond Rd, Dalston to see some of our friends playing in a band called 'The Sheratons'. There was great excitement one weekend when the Sheratons explained that they were recording at the studio of Joe Meek in Holloway Rd, under the management of Ken Howard and Allan Blakely. Each week the excitement grew until the record was finally released. 'The Sheratons' changed their name and 'Have I the Right' went straight to number one in the music charts, not only in England but in twenty seven other countries around the world. We were all celebrating and enjoying basking in the success of the record by the band which was now called 'The Honeycombs'.

The Honeycombs were top of the charts and were in demand everywhere. Dennis, the singer, had a very distinctive voice which added to the group's appeal - especially to the female fans. The Honeycombs were soon continually touring all over the world, and we tried hard to emulate their success back home in England. There were parties when they returned home with loads of stories about their shows and the fun they had playing with other bands - especially 'The Kinks'.

Martin Murray suddenly announced that he had decided to leave the Honeycombs. He was the rhythm guitarist and so Peter Pye was quickly drafted in to take his place and continue with the touring commitments that had been made. The Skylarks went through various changes of personnel after Peter left, I found myself working more and more as a freelance guitarist. Martin Murray then created an artiste management company and subsequently formed 'The Lemmings' with Vic Long, Chris Spooner, Barry Hebb and myself. The Lemmings were basically another incarnation of The Skylarks. There was a lot of financial backing; an office, band clothing and all new Burns instruments and amplifiers. We did a lot of recording, again at the studio of Joe Meek and some at Pye Studios in London's West End. The music written by Martin and played by us was not really to my taste. I liked more of a rock based kind of music and was starting to hear Jimi Hendrix and others playing guitar in a way that I had never heard before. There were high hopes for our records 'Cant blame me for trying' and 'Luverly Luverly' which reached such low positions in the charts as to be embarrassing, and after loads of money had been spent, it was considered that the venture was a flop - at least that is what I called it.

Around this time I was approached by a bass player called Ron Bending. He had a good musical heritage and had played with some top bands and musicians. He had seen me playing in a band at The Bush Hill Park

Tavern and subsequently hired a garage in Carterhatch Lane, Enfield, getting a drummer named Bob and myself along there for a try out session. When the three of us played together the chemistry was evident to us all, and when we finished jamming we just sat around laughing with joy. We had never really met or played together before but it was as if we had been together for years. Ron sung and played bass, Bob was a dynamic drummer, and I just sat on top and rocked away. The music felt great and we could have had a fantastic band but God decided otherwise. We played in pubs and had a regular spot in 'The Brewery Tap' at Ware. The venue was an underground bar, small, sweaty, hot and bags of atmosphere. Bob wanted money and so if a better paying job came in he would not be playing with us for just a few quid, but going off and playing elsewhere for more money. In the very short time we were together we were called 'Kerly Grindalbrite' - I have no idea where this name came from and I don't think the audiences even knew we had a name. Getting a good band together is a bit like baking a perfect cake; timing and ingredients need to be perfect. The three of us worked perfectly together but it was not to be.

My good friend from The Lemmings, Chris Spooner, went on to play bass with Australian chart topping band 'The Mixtures' which had a hit with 'The Pushbike Song'. Chris toured extensively with the band and eventually settled in Australia. It was an awful shock for us all back in England to learn that soon after settling in Australia Chris died in a fishing accident. He had tried to retrieve some fishing equipment from the water where he was fishing, when his waders filled up and pulled him under. Chris was a great character as well as a great bass player and he was missed by everyone so much in Australia and back home here in England.

Then came news that the Honeycombs were reforming with a new line up. Anne Lantree the drummer, and her brother John Lantree who was the bass player, were reforming the band after Dennis D'Ell the singer, Peter Pye and Allan Ward the lead guitarist, were leaving to continue with other projects. I was called in as the new lead guitarist, Colin Boyd was auditioned and became the singer, and Eddie Spencer joined as an all round musician playing keyboards, saxophone and flute. With John and Anne it was a great line up; we all had similar tastes in music and there was plenty of room for freedom of expression, song writing and musical input. The band initially named 'The New Honeycombs', quickly put together various musical sets so that we could play the club scene, the cabaret scene, or simply tour. Publicity shots were taken, new custom made clothing and instruments were acquired - guitars from Burns, amplifiers from Fender and drums from Gretsch. We toured all over the UK and played some gigs and shows in Europe. Some of these shows were filmed for TV and as new members, we felt as though we were now finally successful pop stars.

Whilst playing a number of dates in Belgium we visited a traditional clog maker based in Holland. I was very interested in how wooden clogs could be worn comfortably, and so I bought a few pairs that seemed to fit. I found these clogs to be very comfortable and rather eccentrically started wearing them on a day-to-day basis and on stage during our shows. The brightly coloured clogs became part of my regular stage uniform together with other strange pieces of clothing and decorative objects we collected on our travels.

A long tour of duty was arranged in Israel and we played to packed audiences every evening at the Dan Hotel in Tel Aviv and sometimes in the Dan Hotel at Haifa. During one of our evening performances in Haifa there was a tremendous electrical storm with lightning threatening the circular glass domed concert hall. After one almighty lightning strike the electricity went dead, all the lights went out and our amplifiers were silenced. We sat in the middle of the dance floor with acoustic guitars singing and playing to calm the worried audience as lighted candles were placed on each of the tables. The lightning flashed and the thunder rolled, but we kept on singing and playing while the candles flickered and glowed. That was one of our best ever shows, we got a full standing ovation when the lights eventually went back on.

* * *

We also added big open air shows and theatres to the itinerary and played to some very big audiences. The schedule for playing these extra concerts and shows was quite tight as we rushed from one venue to another. On one occasion we arrived late for a show and had to cut short the music by around ten minutes to get to the next show. The audience rioted with chairs, bottles and seats being thrown at the stage. We made a quick exit via the stage door to our waiting Ford Mustang, where we were surrounded by angry fans who felt that we had cut short the show and given bad value for money. They were right of course, and continued kicking and beating on the car as we drove off through the crowd. The car was ruined, and after that frightening experience we tried to make sure that we played a little longer and if necessary gave an encore, to keep ourselves safe and the audiences happy.

Playing in Israel, with the audience a lttle too close for comfort.

The influences of all of us were injected into the music and my own contributions on the guitar became more and more flamboyant together with the clothes that I wore and the style of playing that I developed. I used feedback and if the ceiling was low enough I would thrust the screaming guitar upwards and into the ceiling. One of the show highlights was our version of Zorba's Dance - nothing like the original, but still exciting and more like a Jimi Hendrix track than anything else. We were riding high on the back of 'Have I the Right' - the Honeycombs Number One hit record from 1964, and together with this and our other original songs, we also included rock and soul music in our shows. The audiences loved it all and we always finished with cheering, stamping and shouting for more. Dressed in Clogs that I picked

up in Holland and custom made brightly coloured clothing that we all wore, audiences were brought to a frenzy,
and indeed we ourselves found it difficult to come down
and resume normality after playing these kind of exciting shows every night.

The after show partying usually went on until
the early hours of the morning, sharing drinks and jokes
with the friends we had made. We became particularly
hungry after one of our late night drinking sessions and
decided to raid the hotel kitchen in search of food.
Everything of course was locked away and the only food
item to be found was a large one gallon tin of strawberry
jam. We started eating the jam with our hands and it was
not long before a jam fight resulted, with splodges of jam
ending up all over the walls and floor of the kitchen. John,
who was in a worse state of inebriation than any of us,
wearing only his underwear, collapsed unconscious onto
the kitchen floor. We decided to decorate him with the
bright red strawberry jam, covering him from head to
foot in the red stickiness. One of us had the idea to move
John into the lift and so we pulled him along the floor
and loaded him still unconscious, into the lift. We then
pressed the button to send him up to the ground floor
reception area. We heard screaming and shouting from
up above as the lift door was opened. People in the reception area waiting to take the lift were shocked to see
an almost naked body in the lift covered in what looked
like blood. It was considered that a horrific murder had
been committed and the Police and emergency services
were called. We got in a lot of trouble over that particular event but the memory of it stays smiling in my mind.

The management of the hotel were perhaps
more lenient with us than we deserved. In all probability

this was because the hotel club and bar where we played every night was always packed out. We had developed a kind of celebrity status and that, together with the music, kept the hotel music bar full and the (very expensive) drinks flowing. We were in the daily papers and on the news and the hotel management loved it.

After we had finished our set at the Dan Hotel one evening, a few of us went out for a 'bender'. We were very drunk and I decided to perform a kind of pole dance around a parking meter. As I swung around, the parking meter became loose and in my state of inebriation, I lifted the meter out of the ground. It was of course top heavy and fell to the ground smashing to pieces and throwing hundreds of coins all over the road. The Police arrived, guns were thrust into our stomachs and we were taken forcibly to the police station and thrown into a cell, which looked more like a dungeon with iron bars. As the hours ticked by we begged for some water. Dehydrated and still partially drunk we sat on the floor of the cell, which was smelly, dirty and hot. For some time our pleas for water were ignored but finally a metal bucket of water was placed on the floor outside of the cell so that we could reach through the bars with a metal cup to obtain some water. Between us we drank the whole bucket of water. By now morning and daylight was approaching and we saw a cleaner arrive. Carrying his mop he calmly picked up our drinking bucket and filled it with water once again - to mop the filthy floor. We had been drinking out of the cleaners bucket used to clean the floors, the cells and the toilets of the police station. Urghhhhh!

The management of the hotel bailed us out and we were free once again. The story (and the pictures) made all of the national newspapers in Israel, not least because we were still wearing stage clothes, jewelry and make up (yes, we wore makeup for fun before the glam-rock fashion started), when the crime was committed. The story was also picked up by the papers in the UK and made embarrassing reading for our families back home. Our shows became even more popular and wherever we went there were requests for autographs or photos.

We often saw a very strange visitor at our shows in the Dan Hotel. Bright blue eyes and skin like the lea-ther of a business man's brown brogue shoes: dressed in just a loin cloth and sandals, and with long white hair and a long white beard, the nearly naked old man would appear, throw his arms in the air and shout "Alleluia." In response the crowd would return the shout in unison; "Alleluia." This would happen three times and then everything would return to normal. It was a fantastic spectacle watching this man who appeared out of no-where and resembled an apparition of Jesus. He would obtain a free drink or two from the bar and then settle down to enjoy the music. When he was ready to leave he stood again, arms in the air, and the three choruses of Al-leluia would be repeated again. After seeing this happen many times I thought I must meet him. He spoke clearly, with an American accent and he seemed very well edu-cated, lucid and intelligent. He invited me to spend some time with him during the following day and so we met on the beach at the rear of the hotel. He was followed by a group of stray dogs which he kept on lengths of string and he proceeded to show me some sea 'fishing'. He had a bent nail on a piece of string which he repeatedly flung into the sea. I suggested using a proper fish hook and some bait. He ignored my suggestion and carried on flinging his line into the sea with obviously no results. We sat on the beach and talked; I was interested in who this old man really was. From our conversation it transpired that Alleluia was an ex American University professor and had probably served time in some war. He must have had some kind of nervous breakdown which resulted in his rather weird behaviour. His words were clear and articulate and he advised me to take fifteen minutes each day to sit quietly and empty my mind, after I explained the pressures of so much playing and the distortion of normal everyday life caused by the popularity and success that we had. He invited me to his home to meet his friend. We walked along the beach to a disused pillbox - a kind of brick reinforced battlement defence built in case of war or attack from the sea. The building was circular and we had to crouch low to enter. There were of course no lights, but a small slice of light entered through a slit in the wall. The smell was awful - dank and acrid, and I wondered how anyone could live in here; a dark damp cell. As my eyes became accustomed to the lack of light I could see a flat concrete bunk and Alleluia then introduced me to his 'friend'. The semi naked body lying on the concrete bunk had a pallid - almost luminous tone and there was no movement, no speech, no sign of breathing. Overcome by nausea I left and made my apologies. I never felt in danger at any time, but was intrigued as to how such a clever person could act in such a bizarre way and live in such an awful manner. He still came back to the Dan Bar for his music and drink, but I often wondered if any others knew what I knew about this very strange and unusual man.

There was one more rather unfortunate incident whilst we were playing in Israel. We were surprised to be given a day off with no work; no clubs or concerts to play during the day or evening. We were all pleased and happy to get a bit of free time, and so we located a car for hire and decided to travel out and see a bit of the country. As we drove through the suburbs of Tel Aviv we noticed that the streets were deserted. No other cars or shoppers were to be seen. Suddenly out of the blue, a brick hit the car windscreen. We skidded to a halt and before we could get out of the car another brick hit the bodywork. From nowhere a crowd of people started throwing stones and shouting at us. We did not understand and quickly drove away whilst more and more people came out into the streets shouting and throwing stones and various other missiles at us. We escaped safely but found out later that we had been given a 'Holy Day' off, a day when people are not allowed to go about their normal life and certainly not allowed to use cars in any way as tourists.

Upon our return to England we made efforts to promote our records. In London's West End, we would wear our stage clothing whilst in public to create some publicity. We hung around various record shops and music shops in Denmark St (Tin Pan Alley) always ending up at La Gioconda coffee shop, frequented by the London music fraternity.

We supported the Moody Blues whilst touring the UK, who had had a big number one hit with their record 'Go Now', at the time when The Beatles were in the charts and on the radio every day. I remember Denny Laine, the singer in the Moody Blues, talking in depth with us back stage about The Beatles and their latest recordings which had not yet been released. Denny was involved in some way with The Beatles and he had heard tracks that had been recorded but not yet released. We sat and listened in disbelief as he described one of the amazing tracks that he had heard, describing it as a kind of children's nursery rhyme about a yellow submarine. At that time the story seemed too far-fetched to be true.

We had again cut a number of tracks at Joe Meek's studio located in his flat above a leather shop in London's Holloway Road. I had recorded there a little in the past and so I kind of 'knew' him and knew of his very strange temperament and mood changes. He gave us a lot of time and freedom in the studio with our arrangements, but in return got us to record a few of his songs. Joe was very experimental and after hearing me playing around using my metal comb to slide up and down the guitar fretboard, he used the idea on one of his songs; 'Should a Man Cry.' We did some great experimental guitar effects on some of the tracks recorded in the studio, some were released but I don't know what became of many of those recordings. After his tragic death hundreds of tapes were removed from the studio and stored in tea chests. These tapes subsequently became know as the 'Tea Chest Tapes' and some have even been released.

When there was time and when Joe was in one of his 'good moods', we were encouraged to experiment further musically. One of the strangest ideas recorded was a story we invented, filled with jokes and innuendo together with musical sound effects - a sort of Monty Python story set to music. It must have been good, I remember how we all laughed at the tape playback.

Joe thought a lot of us and the efforts we made inside and outside of the studio. He was however a manic depressive and one could never know just what kind of mood he would be in. A studio session may have been booked and Joe would shout down the stairs from his flat - "Fuck Off" as we banged on the door to gain entry and take our equipment upstairs to the studio. The following day we would arrive again and he would sweetly great us all as if nothing had happened. There were drugs, depression and homosexuality in Joe's life which we all ignored, but it was still a terrible shock when he shot his landlady and then shot and killed himself during one of his depressive rages. I had heard him ranting previously about 'the fucking landlady' and 'the rent.' He certainly was a gifted record producer with number one hits such as 'Telstar' in the UK and the USA, and he was the innovator of many studio sound effects that are still used today. He used an old upright piano which had drawing pins on each of the piano hammers giving the piano a honky tonk kind of jangly sound. The floor of the recording studio was thick with tape; discarded offcuts from his reel-to-reel tape machines. There was echo from a mike placed in an upstairs bathroom, double tracking and the speeding up of voices, instruments or backing tracks; all were techniques invented and regularly used by Joe.

One of our favourite haunts in London was Imhoffs in New Oxford St. The large record store stocked all of our records and so we would often go in to create a buzz, helping to publicise The Honeycombs and our latest record release. It was in this store that I met my first wife, Rita, who often helped with my requests for American record imports, which were not generally available in the UK. We both shared a great love of music and were married in 1968.

The Honeycombs newer records that were released did not make a very big impact. After the great response we had abroad and particularly in Israel, we returned to England to discover that the Honeycombs finances were in poor shape and there was no money left to pay any of us. It was hard to accept, but unfortunately none of us had any real financial, legal or contractual knowledge or skill. In fact we were so busy enjoying the music, the fun and the touring that we were not bothered about those kinds of things. I later found out that my income tax and National Insurance contributions that should have been paid by the Honeycombs accountant, were never ever paid at all, and I ended up having to pay a lot of overdue tax and National Insurance arrears. The accountant disappeared, never to be seen again and the Honeycombs gradually parted ways, all of us broke.

The irony does however continue; almost 50 years after these events, Martin Murray, one of the original members, has reformed the Honeycombs with a new line up of members. He is of course the only original member and now at 70 plus he is on the road once again! It only happens in Rock n' Roll!

A Honeycombs publicity shot featured in a German Magazine

WHAT HAPPENED?

'It's Rock n Roll man' - Keith Richards

A s the Honeycombs were winding down to a natural exit from the pop world, the relationship with my future wife Rita took over most of my interest. I tried to become more conventional (a process most difficult for me) wearing a jacket or suit and tie. I tried to stop some of my playful antics and practical jokes which I knew annoyed her (and most of the opposite sex). There was always an intangible tense atmosphere or vibe between my Mum and Rita. I ignored it but I knew that there was something not clicking. I got on with her Mum and Dad well and they were both very kind to me. As the months dissolved, we became engaged with a view to getting married. Marriage was something that I had never previously considered; for one thing, my life on the road with various bands and groups was not compatible with married life and being settled down. I had to get a job and try to obtain some sort of regular income with a view to buying a home. I looked for a job that once again came with a car, which I considered would save a considerable amount of money, that I would not have to fork out for petrol, tax and insurance. The one job that I found in the local paper that seemed to have a car as part of its attraction, was based in Sunbury on Thames - miles away. The job itself was for a 'Window Display Representative', and was advertised by Gartside Window Display Organisation. 'Window Display Representative' was just a posh way of saying 'window dresser' or 'display person' but whichever way the job was described I had no experience, knowledge or skill in this field whatsoever. Having no experience as a display representative did not seem like a reasonable excuse not to apply for the job (and the car), and so I got my best togs out and found my way by train to Sunbury on Thames for the job interview.

The company had large offices and a selection of small studios where clients could be shown the impressive skills of the company display reps. After a brief interview with the usual questions; have you any display experience? 'Yes'. can you drive? 'Yes'. 'Where would you like to see yourself in six months time? etc. etc. I was asked to complete a window display in one of the studios. Ah! Big problem I thought. I cannot do displays. The boss of the company told me to complete a display whilst he was away for his one hour lunch. I sat down and considered the matter in hand, with no idea what to do or how to approach the display.

The display that I was required to complete was a wine and beer display for a chain of brewers. I took a sneak look in the other studios to see what kind of thing was possible, and then going back to my own studio, I tried to replicate what I had seen in the other studios. What I created looked awful; nothing like the other professionally designed displays that I had craftily looked at and copied from. The hour was nigh! The company boss Mr Gartside senior himself, returned to look at my work. He stood back and held his chin with one hand, saying nothing. He must have stood there silently for at least one minute. Finally I could stand the silence no more and asked

"Well, what do you think of my work?"

His answer was simple; "I have seen a lot better, but I have also seen a lot worse." I was offered the job and was to start the following week (probably because there were so few applicants for the position.)

My first week of work was to be a week of training with the company's top display man, Bernard Rowland. Bernard lived in Woolwich, South London, and so every morning I had to make the journey to arrive at his house by 8.30am, ready to accompany him to his first job of the day. My company car was a blue Austin A35 van and I found that it was capable of achieving good speeds doing up to 85 miles per hour, leaving home at 7.00am each morning to reach Woolwich by 8.30am via empty roads and of course the Woolwich Ferry across the Thames.

Bernard was extremely artistic and creative and it was easy to pick up his display themes, techniques and ideas. He was what I would call a natural window dresser; feminine and a lovely chap to boot! Bernard was inspirational, with a simplicity of style in the design of his work; I admired him working quickly and creatively and couldn't wait to get out on my own and try to create some good displays. The displays themselves featured a centerpiece with other related products displayed in an artistic manner in the window. The whole display was supported with a crepe paper background, with flares and tubes of stretched crepe paper giving the window display an attractive and colourful appearance. Bernard began each job by putting a handful of metal tacks in his mouth, ejecting them one by one onto a magnetic hammer, and tacking the crepe paper into place – this was all done in one smooth movement, with the crepe paper layered and stretched into place very quickly. I learnt that this was the old technique of how window dressers and display artists used to work, and it was explained to me that I would have a mechanical staple gun to do the work. I was certainly glad I didn't have to put metal tacks in my mouth to complete each window display. Bernard joked, that after accidentally swallowing a mouthful of these tacks, it certainly made a mess of his underpants! It was a unique experience, and I was probably watching the very last of these old style display artists in action. I was not just watching display history, but learning lessons that would help and support me greatly in future years.

Each job had a docket with the job address and details of what type of display was required. I created displays in my time at Gartside's for a wide range of companies and their products; Avon and Firestone Tyres, Bemax, Helena Rubenstein cosmetics, Ind Coope Beers - Long Life, Skol, Double Diamond, Callard and Bowser sweets, Suchard chocolates, Cow and Gate baby food, Royal Birthday and Christmas cards, Regency Wines and many, many more. I learnt a lot about sales, marketing, advertising and of course window displays.

The job at Gartsides set me up financially. As well as the job and the car I made contacts with many in the marketing business and did lots of private work at weekends and during the evenings. At Christmas time there was lucrative work installing Christmas decorations in pubs. The decorations were made at home using crepe paper, scissors and a sewing machine, with two or even three pubs decorated in one day, often working in the pubs before and after opening and closing times. I was very successful in getting the pubs to sign up for their Christmas decorations to be installed. The pub landlords in turn recommended me to other pub managers and I became busier and busier during the weeks leading up to Christmas. The Boleyn Tavern, The Pearly Queen, The Higham Hill Tavern, The Green Man, The Blind Beggar, The Crooked Billet and many of the well known East London pubs booked me up months in advance to put up their Christmas decorations, all made at home out of crepe paper using an old borrowed Singer sewing machine. The Christmas decorations were part of an old East London pub tradition where the decorations were installed a couple of weeks before Christmas and ripped down by the merry makers taking part in the celebrations when the clock struck twelve on New Years Eve. 'Health and Safety' has now of course banned the use of such paper decorations, however, I never ever heard of a fire starting because of this tradition.

In one year £1000 was accumulated, enough for a deposit on 28 Dimsdale Drive in Enfield. The total cost was £5,250.00; it doesn't seem much now but in those days it was a fortune.

Rita and I were married 29th June 1968 at St Stephens Church and moved in to our new home - 28 Dimsdale Drive at Bush Hill Park. My old friend Bimbo assisted in demolishing walls, knocking out chimneybreasts and generally reconstructing the property. Improvements were made continually, with pine cladding for the kitchen, together with a modern breakfast bar that I designed and built myself. A futuristic design was painted on the walls of the lounge, concealed lighting and built in wardrobes for the bedroom. Old fashioned chimney breasts were removed and central heating installed. New picture windows were fitted upstairs and downstairs and it seemed that the activity of improving and decorating never ended.

Our son Daren was born in 1969 and a few years in 1976 later our lovely baby daughter Simone arrived too. I enjoyed those early years of childhood greatly, doing all of the usual parental things that are as much fun for the parents as the children. Football, skateboarding and biking were Daren's favourite activities. Simone enjoyed the park and going on the swings, slide and roundabout. She would insist on using the larger sets of apparatus rather than the smaller ones used by other little children of her age. She had extreme confidence, in fact confidence to the point of being dangerous.

There were of course the normal parental worries; Simone sitting in a supermarket shopping trolly decided to stand up, she overbalanced and fell head first onto the supermarket floor. There was silence for a few moments while she lay there unmoving and then an ear-splitting scream followed by tears and a visit to the hospital where it was concluded that there was no real damage. One day after a school event and aged just seven, she walked the mile journey home across the Cambridge Road (the A10) after being missed at the school pick up point. The panic that a parent feels when a child has gone missing is indescribable. The dangers; there are so many of them. Crossing a busy main road that ran alongside the school, navigation of a railway line via a footbridge, crossing traffic lights in a main road to reach the busy A10 – The Great Cambridge Rd, where accidents involving cars, motorbikes, and pedestrians happened daily. Finally, in Bury St West, Tears streaming, unable to talk, I found her walking home alone, after Police, friends and relatives had all been contacted. So many emotions run through a parent's mind when something like that happens.

Daren of course was not immune to the accidents that parents of children witness; running in the front garden and falling headfirst onto the front gate spearing his forehead with a large rusty screw sticking out of the woodwork was one of the worst. Holding him down on a hospital bed while the nurse stitched his head back together was worse still. A little older and on his bike, he cycled into a thick wire invisibly stretched across two gate posts nearly detaching his head from his body. Parenting is not easy, as most children will eventually discover.

Daren enjoyed games and water fun in the back garden. I would sometimes build an assault course with ladders and planks of wood leading to the inflatable paddling pool. This was one of the favourite Summer garden activities, and always resulted in everyone within a few yards proximity getting soaked. Daren also liked model toys, soldiers and space monsters. One day we created a short film using some of these toy models that were connected to and operated by lengths of cotton thread, then lifted and moved in various directions. We filmed the action using an old 'Super 8' cine camera. Sound effects were included and I remember the film entertaining everyone as it was projected onto a portable screen erected in the lounge or 'front room.'

During this rather chaotic time, and before Simone was born, Gartside Window Display Organisation decided to make all of its employees self-employed, and thus reduce a lot of their expenditure on employment as the fortunes of the company slowly declined. This gave me a lot more freedom to program my work as I wished, it also gave me more time to work on my ambitions in the music business. While Daren was still a toddler, and before Simone was born, I took Rita and him 'on the road' with me. 'The Gill James Invasion' had recruited me as their guitarist and had loads of good paying work lined up. I did however, need some new professional equipment to get started in this new venture. Albert, my cousin's husband, owned a beautiful Gibson Les Paul SG guitar, I made him an offer to buy it and prepared to get myself a Marshall 'stack' (an essential stack of two 4 x 12 speaker units). The band worked for some time in the Newcastle and Sunderland areas of North East England, playing at lots of venues on the 'Mecca' circuit. We supported bands like Slade, Genesis, Medicine Head and even David Bowie. It was not of course an ideal family situation, although Daren seemed to enjoy being the mascot for the band and meeting lots of the other musicians that we worked with. He used to enjoy sitting on the revolving stage that a lot of the Mecca venues used to feature the supporting band and then the headliner. My work did create tensions and problems in the family, and consequently I gradually lost interest in the band which mainly performed other people's hit songs. I did have quite a bit of spare time during the day and this was the time I started writing my own material. I felt that to get anywhere in the music business, a band had to have something new and original to offer and not just be a 'cover band' playing hits from the charts.

I still had my ambition for success in the music business and one day received a call from an old friend

Vic Long. He had secured a regular spot in a pub in Camden Town and needed a guitarist to complete the band's line up. The job was a regular payer, but the loud rock music we played was not really suitable for the venue. We were playing there regularly but Vic soon stopped enjoying the pub job and decided to quit the band and the gig. I tried to keep the job going with various changes in band personnel. Although I took over the job of vocalist in the band, I was never a good singer and we soon received our marching orders from the pub residency, probably due to my own substandard vocals. We then joined forces with Billie Ritchie who played keyboards and took over as vocalist. We changed the name of the band to 'X' and confused most of the audiences we played to with our unusual style of rock/poetry, much of which Billie had written. The band did well and played lots of gigs in London, including the famous 'Marquee', at that time based in Wardour St. 'X' recorded quite a few tracks written by Billie and some, particularly 'Madhouse', met with critical acclaim from within the music business. One of our regular gigs was at 'The Pearly Queen' (more recently called 'The Hayloft' and now a paint shop) in East London's Mile End Road. Steve, an old Newcastle friend, had taken over management of the pub and he insisted that live music should be played almost every night. The times that we played there were like enormous party nights. The pub would be packed and the music was loud. At 11.00pm, when everyone was pretty merry, the doors would be locked and we would carry on the party. The parties went on until the early hours of the morning, but unbeknown to anyone, we were being watched by staff who worked at night and lived on the top floor of the Charrington's brewery on the opposite side of the road. One day the brewery management arrived, took the keys and the cash from the till, whilst Steve and his girlfriend were unceremoniously dumped with their cases and belongings on the pavement outside. That was the end of that gig, but I still smile if I ever have cause to pass through that area.

Slowly but surely 'X' disintegrated, and once again I found myself with a bass player and drummer, even more acutely aware of the band's vocal weakness. The band continued with 'Izzy' on bass and drummer Tom Compton and I started my own brand of rock music with my own vocals. The excitement was there and the music was wild and I gradually gained more confidence in my own vocals with the help of a 'Copycat' Echo machine! but something was missing and it was not just the vocals. We gained a good following mainly because we were very strong instrumentally, using the influences of Jimi Hendrix and Carlos Santana to create an exciting and unusual sound. We were called 'Bang' and we were very proud of the music and the following we gained. However, we needed better vocals, original material and a personality. Having spoken to the other band members it was decided to approach an old friend; one who could sing and one who was a great 'front man'. Dennis D'Ell, the singer from the Honeycombs, was the man that I really wanted in the band. Apart from his talent, I knew that he was totally professional and his presence in the band would propel us to further success. I had a meeting with Dennis, and whilst I was holding my breath waiting for his response to the proposition, he casually agreed and said smiling;

"I was waiting for you to ask me."

He thought it was a great idea. I couldn't hide my

excitement.

I had been writing songs for some time and Dennis took these songs and put his own stamp and character onto the music and the words. Demo tapes were made and we soon found ourselves a recording manager by the name of Miki Dallon. Miki's company, 'Pilot Music', took us into various studios in London, Wembley and Kent to record and mix our songs. The songs sounded great with Dennis singing them and we all felt as though we were on to something big. Some of the recordings, however, did not go too well, and it soon became evident that the drummer, who was varying the tempo, was the weak point. The drummer (with a little encouragement), left the band and together we approached one of the greatest drummers around at that time - Harry Hughes. I was now punching well above my weight with Dennis on vocals and Harry on drums. Harry was originally in a very successful and innovative rock band with Billie Ritchie called 'Clouds'. We benefitted greatly when Harry agreed to join our band and take over drumming on our unfinished tracks. I have always believed that a band is only as good as it's drummer, and Harry certainly lifted and inspired us all to new heights when we played or recorded together. Dennis coined the band's name - 'Zarabanda' - and the recordings now went into overdrive, with power house drummer Harry driving us all forward. 'Living on the Line', 'Midnight Lady', 'Run with the Crowd', 'Let me down easy', 'Rain on the Roof' and dozens of my other songs were recorded with Dennis on vocals, Harry on drums and Izzy on bass, it was a great line up and when we started doing live shows the audiences couldn't get enough. The moral of this is of course; a band is only as good as the drummer.

I should explain that this period of time was generally known as the hippie or drug culture period. Drugs have always been evident in the music business and years ago when I first went on the road, 'Purple Hearts' and 'Black Bombers' were in daily use by many musicians and band members. Nothing had really changed since then, and in spite of the dangers, drugs of all kinds were everywhere and everyone seemed to be experimenting with mixing various kinds of drugs. Of course the music industry was awash with drugs, and it was common knowledge that the Stones and the Beatles had experimented and tried most of what was available. Marijuana or hash was the usual drug being regularly used. Cocaine was a more expensive and more 'up-market' kind of drug. A friend in the USA sent us some 'Sunshine' or LSD directly through the post, and the trips we took on this drug were amazing and sometimes very frightening. After my own experiences with LSD, cocaine and marijuana I would not recommend any of them to be used at all. I was very lucky to come away from drug use unharmed, but there were fatalities, and I lost one very good musician friend, Richard Osbourne, through the use of drugs. Richard had to be helped onto the stage some nights and his hands placed on the keyboard of his piano. He couldn't focus on much at all during those drug fuelled nights and he died a year or two later. Richard was a great musician playing saxophone, flute and keyboards - such a terrible waste. Many other people in the music world have lost their lives to drugs, including my all-time guitar hero, Jimi Hendrix and of course others such as Elvis Presley and Michael Jackson, and more recently Amy Winehouse. I believe that all drugs, no matter in what quantities, are harmful and, to many, lethal. I don't really understand that with the music so good, we needed any kind of chemical additions to enhance our joy and excitement. However, I was to become pivotally involved in the drugs and music scene.

Having a horticultural background, I was naturally interested in the seeds that were often found in supplies of marijuana. I attempted to propagate some of these, and to my surprise they germinated and quickly grew into sturdy little window plants. Wanting to take the experiment a little further, I transplanted these seedlings into the back garden and with a very hot summer the plants grew and grew and grew. Flowering heads (the most important part of the marijuana plant), appeared and the plants continued growing upwards, eventually reaching some ten to twelve feet in height. During all of this time we were harvesting the crop and making very good (and enjoyable) use of it. Leaves were the size of dinner plates and these would often be ripped off from the plant and boiled up to make us a nice pot of 'tea'. Flowering heads were dried and later on smoked.

Friends heard about my 'crop' and often arrived asking for a supply. I was happy to oblige but I put a stop to this when people that I didn't know started telephoning and offering large amounts of money for bags of marijuana. I did not want to become known as a drug dealer with all the problems that that would bring. I was happy to give some of the crop to friends but didn't want to be involved in trafficking or selling drugs although money was offered.

My garage in the garden had been converted into a soundproofed studio where I wrote most of my songs. Zarabanda also used the studio to rehearse and prepare for recording or putting on live shows. There were always musicians in the house or the garage making music and smoking our own home grown 'weed'. Looking back, this was not a good environment in which to bring up two young children, and it is not really surprising that both of them have gone into the music business, although this was not something I purposely encouraged. All of the musicians enjoyed seeing the children and in fact the musicians became part of our extended family. It was a fun time, but again I would not endorse any kind of drug use or this kind of environment to bring children up in. I believe that marijuana makes one very lethargic, and continuous use discourages almost any kind of activity outside of the user's own immediate personal pleasure, or should I say, escape. It was certainly true that I had to finish completely with any kind of drugs or drink when I started Karate. The two just did not work together. Concentration and discipline are required for any of the Martial Arts, and it may be that starting Karate at this time actually took me away from drugs and saved my life.

As well as the rock music pubs that Zarabanda was regularly playing in, we often filled empty dates by playing in variety shows during times when work was thin. A promoter would organise a show that featured a comedian, a magician, a male or female stripper and some music. We would play at these events, often providing the backing music for a guest singer or even sometimes the strippers. One day we were booked onto a hen party, and after bringing in all of our equipment and setting it up, we watched, hidden as the ladies arrived. They all looked very demure, well made up and fashionable, and I thought how difficult it must be to entertain a few hundred females on a show like this. The compere did his bit by exciting the audience and introducing the comedian. We backed the guest singer and played a few songs of our own, but after a while the audience became impatient for the star of the show - the male stripper. In the changing room we listened to the stamping, banging and shouting for the main star of the show. The male stripper that had been booked had not yet arrived. The compere rushed into the room in a panic. He was fearing for his life!

"If the stripper doesn't arrive soon I've had it."

He was genuinely frightened that the audience of ladies who were now standing on the tables shouting, would attack him. The noise got louder and he started begging one of us to be the stripper for the show. There is a certain amount of confidence required in standing in front of 300 women and whipping ones kit off - its a very specialised kind of occupation, and none of us were prepared to help the poor man. He struggled back on stage again, explaining that there would be a little more delay before the main event. Bottles and plates were thrown at him and he dived off stage and into the dressing room once again.

"Fifty pounds for any one of you who will go on stage and take you clothes off."

We all started daring Dennis to do it. He refused at first, but after us all bullying him and calling him a wimp, he reluctantly agreed. There was a proviso though. He agreed to go out there with no clothes on if he could wear his guitar - strap lowered so that the instrument covered all of his vital parts. The compere agreed and Dennis was genuinely and naturally petrified. From inside the dressing room the shouting and banging sounded deafening as Dennis removed all of his clothes and put the guitar around his neck. We all tried to build up Dennis's confidence in the changing room by making positive comments about the size of his manhood and shouting "Go Den Go!." He opened the door a few inches, the audience saw the bare skin and erupted into applause. Dennis was sweating heavily and at that exact point the real stripper arrived with his little make up bag – "So sorry I'm late boys" - already with his stage gear and make up on. His name was 'Bubbles'. Of course he was gay (most of them were). Dennis fell to the floor with relief and looked like he had won the football pools, he was so happy. We all erupted in fits of laughter and got completely drunk before we went back on stage again that evening.

I was still working on a self-employed basis for Gartside's but the work became rather spasmodic and so I decided to look for another job. The pay from just playing in the band was not very good and so I began a full time job working at Civic Stores (now gone) in Edmonton, doing similar work to that which I did years previously at Langham Radio. The main difference now was that I had to lift fridges, freezers and washing machines as part of my daily routine, and collect and deliver them for after sales service. Items sold from the shop had to be delivered, sometimes to tower blocks in the Edmonton or Tottenham area. I did, however, have full evening and weekend use of the company's Ford Transit van, which assisted greatly in getting to and from gigs with Zarabanda during evenings and weekends.

After working there for some months, I went in one morning to find the manageress in tears; the bailiffs were taking an inventory of all stock, they closed the shop and kicked the manageress (who was totally dedicated to her job) and her family, out of the company flat where they lived upstairs. Civic Stores had gone into liquidation and this was the end of the road for all of us who worked there.

In 1979 I became involved with Mick Kaminski, through a bass player named Paul Mann. Mick was the violinist in 'The Electric Light Orchestra' and had put together a small offshoot band called 'Violinski'. A record had been produced and the record company wanted to see some action from the band. Mick hurriedly put together a band and drafted me in to play guitar with Paul Mann on bass. I learnt the music quickly and we did various bits of filming and video shoots. The record 'Clogdance' was released and it slowly climbed the charts and just about made the 'Top Ten'. We were booked for Top of the Pops (one of the main TV music shows at that time), and had some great fun with the other acts all on the same show. I remember The Jam, Showaddywaddy, Rolf Harris, Lena Lovitch and a few others that were all on that same show. Eventually the record dropped out of the charts fairly rapidly and Mick continued with his own career in ELO.

I then began a new job working for 'Topic Displays' in West London with a great group of young, creative and dynamic people. The work was similar to that which I did at Gartside's, but this time I was promoting and displaying music - albums and sometimes books. After working there for about a year, all of the employees were called into the office at 9.00am one morning. We were simply told to hand over the keys of our company cars to the liquidators of the company. It happened again! I was beginning to think that it was me putting a jinx onto the companies that I worked for!

At home, the giant marijuana plants still growing along the length of the garden did create quite a bit of interest. The next door neighbour, Harry, a kindly old man, saw the plants growing way above the garden fence and often asked me what the plants were, did they have flowers or fruit of any kind? I had to reply with the lie that "they were weeds and they had sprung up of their own accord."

Two police officers arrived on the front doorstep one day. They asked to come in and there was no option but to sit them down in the room facing onto the back garden. The enquiries were about Steve, a friend who had been committing various misdemeanours. The police wanted to know of his whereabouts, but we of course did not tell them that he was in fact lodging with us at that time. (Steve was in fact the ex-manager of the Pearly Queen). As the enquiries proceeded, one of the officers continually looked out into the garden, he seemed to be very interested in the large strange plants growing there. I felt a rising panic and tried to bring his attention back to within the room, offering cups of tea and biscuits. Eventually the enquiries finished and the police left. I considered that the house would shortly be invaded by the drug squad and telephoned Dennis to help me rip the plants out and dump them. Driving from his home in Brentwood, he arrived thirty minutes later after I had started ripping all of the offending plants out. He was adamant that we should not dump the plants but save them and dry them out for use in the future. I reasoned that I had to get them away from the house as the police might return, and it was agreed that the plants would be broken up and put in Dennis's car to be driven back to his home. At that time Dennis owned a Volkswagen Beetle and we crammed a dozen giant marijuana plants into his car. The only thing that could be seen was Dennis's face at the windscreen. The car was packed tight with the plants as I followed him back to Brentwood to help him unload the precious cargo and haul it up into his loft. I believe that the whole of the music industry survived for the next two years as a result of this crop. The drug squad never arrived and the police never returned, but the lodger, Steve, was eventually tracked down and taken in by the police.

Zarabanda was still doing well. The shows were successful everywhere, our records were released in Europe and there was the possibility of a major American record company being interested in signing us up for a record deal. I was flown over to New York to create a bit of interest from the radio stations. One or two of our songs would be played and then I would be interviewed to give some background information on how the band was formed and where we were playing etc. Some of these radio stations were on college campuses and I was often asked to introduce records that were to be played; I think they enjoyed my London accent.

After arriving back in England, I presented the band with a couple more songs that I had completed. 'United State' and 'Living in this world' which I considered were my best two songs to date. We recorded them and everyone felt the excitement of something new and original. Up to that point I had just signed all of the songs over to Miki Dallon's Pilot Music, we had received no payment or advance for record royalties. I did not want to sign over further songs unless we had something concrete to base our optimism on, not money but some kind of contract guaranteeing the band a proper recording future. Miki Dallon had taken on the services of

Jim Giantonio, a small time New York manager, with a view to him securing the deal with Casablanca Records. It did not happen. Miki was asking for an advance that was completely unrealistic for an unknown band and we were left with no recording deal, but we were nevertheless expected to keep on producing songs and records without any plan or contract. I refused to sign over the two latest songs and the situation became stalemate.

Zarabanda continued playing live shows but the recording stopped. 'On the road' with Zarabanda was an extremely enjoyable experience, and Dennis became like a brother to me, always encouraging my efforts and supporting me during the difficult times that every band has.

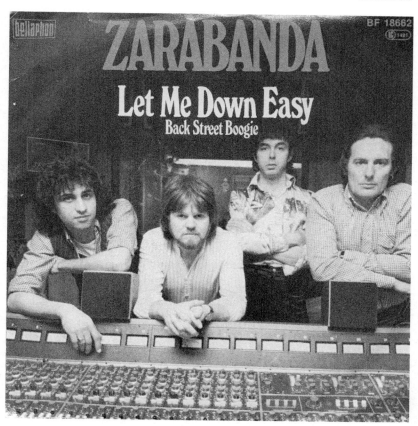

Zarabanda in the studio
Izzy, Harry Hughes, myself and Dennis D'Ell

BEGINNING
KARATE

'If at first you don't succeed try, try, try again'

It was 1977. I had started to take Daren my son to Karate classes. The club in Winchmore Hill, was instructed by the late Mick Randall, one of the very first exponents of Shotokan Karate in England. Daren was 6 or 7 years old and took to the classes easily. I used to stay and sit with the other parents and rather reluctantly watch him in the class, although I couldn't understand the moves or the blocks and punches and how they were supposed to work. After a couple of weeks, the punches and blocks were put together and the class began some sparring exercises. Now it all made sense! I enquired as to whether I was too old to start and was told to come along to the next lesson and enrol.

I was not a natural. My arms and legs would not do as they were instructed. My right leg moved forward instead of my left. My fist was loosely hanging at my side instead of being placed firmly on my hip. I couldn't punch, I couldn't balance. I was never going to emulate Bruce Lee, seen in the films that were so popular at that time. I was in a class with around a dozen lads at least ten years my junior. They all picked the moves up quickly, I struggled and became more and more frustrated with my own inability to assimilate the techniques. I questioned why others in the class seemed to execute the moves so fluidly and effectively whilst I found everything so difficult. At each class I went in more determined than ever, but always came out feeling as if the techniques of Karate would always be elusive to me. Why couldn't I do it when all of the others could? I was determined to improve and found that the discipline and concentration required motivated me to continue.

I discovered that Dennis's brother Laurie, practiced Karate and was in fact a brown belt. We met up and talked enthusiastically about Karate and the Martial Arts, and I was encouraged to travel over to Lol's (Laurie's) house at Hainault every Saturday morning for some extra Karate practice. We practiced 'freestyle' or sparring, and being a beginner, Lol kicked and punched me all around his garden. I learnt how to move (and how to block his head high kicks). He also helped to teach me the first two kata - Kihon Kata and Heian Shodan. After an hour or so, he would let me sit down and rest whilst he practiced and demonstrated some of the higher grade katas. I remember being very interested and impressed by watching Lol perform the unusual Tekki Shodan, and some of the other Kata that I had never seen or heard of before. His movements were sharp and focused and unlike anything I had seen in my own white belt class. I respected Lol and envied the Karate skill that he demonstrated to me in his garden every Saturday morning.

Daren and I both took our first grading at the Picketts Lock Sports Centre in Edmonton (now gone) in 1978. There were hundreds of students taking part in the training and later on, attempting the grading. It seemed as though we waited for hours before being called up to perform. I was nervous for Daren who was called up first. He was also nervous but managed to complete the test requirements without too much difficulty. Later on, my name was called and I was shaking with fear. As I completed the first five stepping punches of the grading, I skidded on the sweaty floor and landed on my backside. Everyone was laughing at the examiners table, and after that embarrassing moment, my nerves disappeared. I considered that I could not do anything quite as bad as that, and so I had nothing to lose. We both subsequently passed our first Karate grading, but soon after that, Daren lost interest and packed up. I could see the benefits of children and adults practising Karate, but I could not get him to return. At that point he was more interested in skateboards and bikes. I stubbornly did not want to be beaten by the challenges of Karate that I found so difficult, and so decided to continue.

One by one, the young guys at the Winchmore Hill club who started Karate classes with me, dropped off and missed their classes. We still met up for drinks in the 'Stag and Hounds' after the Karate class; they just didn't bother to go to the class before going to the pub! I was amazed that they stopped attending the classes and I think they were surprised that I carried on.

I realised that I needed more classes, as some of the classes at Winchmore Hill clashed with the evenings that Zarabanda was playing. I changed clubs and started at Picketts Lock where the classes were on Sunday mornings and Wednesday evenings, times when Zarabanda rarely had any commitments. I found these more advanced Karate classes extremely tough. There were no real dojo rules as such in those early days and it was expected that there would be the occasional black eye or cracked rib. No one ever complained about their injuries - it was not the done thing to complain. We were actually proud of our injuries and didn't feel ashamed that we had been injured as a result of our own misjudgment. There was a very strict hierarchy between the grades; I remember as a yellow belt asking one of the brown belts a question before the class began. He just looked at me and sneered like an aggressive dog without answering. Black and brown belts would regularly beat us lower grades up when we were used for 'freestyle sparring' during a fifteen minute warm up at the beginning of each lesson. I was lifted off of the floor by a Mae Geri (front kick) and landed, winded, on my backside. The Black belt just told me to get up and carry on. I did, and took quite a few more rather painful kicks. One of the favourite tricks of the Black Belts was to sweep your front leg away with an Ashi barai (leg sweep) and then bring their heel crashing down onto your chest (Kakato Geri) whilst you were on the floor. This technique injured a lot of people and gradually our large group of beginners and lower grades got smaller and smaller. No one actually complained but a lot of very good students just didn't bother going along to the classes.

As a result of my extra Saturday morning workout with Lol in his garden, I discovered how to avoid these leg sweeps by turning the attacker round and punching him in the back of the head or the kidneys. This technique worked and my attackers were always shocked with a punch in the back when they tried this technique. I became more confident and maybe a bit cocky too. I just kept going to the classes and never missed. If I ever missed a class I told myself that I had failed and failed through fear or weakness.

On one Winter Sunday morning there were no buses, and cars could not use the roads because there was a very thick snow fall during the night. I put my bag on my back and walked the couple of miles through the snow to the dojo, which was then situated at Picketts Lock Sports Centre in Edmonton. The journey took more than one hour and when I arrived I found a message taped to the dojo door 'NO CLASS TODAY BECAUSE OF SNOW'. I was annoyed but pleased that I had made it when others had not.

Me as a novice 4th Kyu student practising in the garden.

Things were changing. I found that I really looked forward to the Karate classes each week together with my visits to Hainault for extra practice every Saturday. On Saturday evenings Zarabanda was always playing - sometimes a long distance away from home, and the late nights and heavy drinking did not auger well for my regular 10.00am Karate class on Sunday mornings. As Dennis started doing some solo work to supplement his income, the gigs for Zarabanda became less and less until eventually we stopped working as a band. Zarabanda was Dennis's pride and joy. We all got on well and the chemistry that is so important in a band, was always there. We all felt sorry that things had not worked out better for us all.

Dennis and I kept in touch after Zarabanda finished and years later I attended his 60th birthday party - a wonderful surprise party where he sang with his daughter while his son played the guitar. Of course he asked me if I had brought my guitar to the party, I had, and I surprised him by playing a couple of songs with him and his family. I didn't see him again but went to his funeral a couple of years later. I was proud to have known him and proud to have been part of his life and his music. A dear brother who made life so much fun and made music so good.

I felt as though I had given everything possible to become successful in the music business, I had given it my best shot and now it was time to settle down. I had some contacts from my previous work and decided to work as a freelance display merchandiser. The problem was I didn't have much money and again I didn't have a car. Luckily, a neighbour who was in the process of buying a new car kindly offered me his old car at a very nice price - free! What a bargain! It was an enormous old black Vauxhall Victor. It had bench front seating, red leather upholstery and a column gear change, it was not the sort of car that was particularly desirable, but I loved it, and for a couple of years travelled the length and breadth of England and Wales installing displays in record shop windows using my old Vauxhall Victor. I would work my way out through Slough and Reading, finishing my day in

Bristol. After an overnight stay in a guest house, I would drive over the Severn Bridge and do Swansea, Cardiff and a few other Welsh towns. The following day it would be Exeter, Torquay, Paignton and so on all along the South coast. I would then do the same kind of trip in another direction; Leicester, Coventry, Birmingham or Colchester, Norwich, Ipswich, and so on. I earned loads of money and worked hard while the work was there. It wasn't long before my efforts were noticed and I was 'head hunted' by Warner Bros Music - WEA, working directly for them and promoting only Warner Bros. artists. But that's another story.

Being self-employed, I had the freedom to work when I liked, fitting everything around my own Karate training and occasional music jobs that came my way. I found it very hard to escape from playing guitar and the music business that I loved, and when a new lucrative music job came along from 'Pizza Hut', I took it making sure that my Karate days of Wednesdays and Sundays were not put at risk.

The Pizza Hut company had opened a new restaurant in Queensway, West London. They wanted to experiment using live music, and the Queensway branch was to be their flagship music restaurant. I was given a budget that allowed me to supply the sound equipment and hire one or two other musicians, with total jurisdiction over the content of the live music in the restaurant. The music was to be played downstairs in a really nice cellar bar. A small stage was erected and the venue was called 'Pizza Petes'. The job was great. The cellar had great acoustics and was usually packed out with music loving tourists who were visiting or lodging in the area. I used various musical line ups for the shows - sometimes a drummer, sometimes another guitarist, sometimes a sax or flute player. A lot depended on who was available, but as I had to provide the music six nights a week, there was always a supply of good musicians coming and going, filling in on their spare nights with a gig at Pizza Petes when they were not working in their own bands or on other projects.

My good friend the late Derek Dampier was often in the line up playing drums. Another good friend, the late Richard Osbourne, often played Keyboards, Sax or flute with me. Dennis from Zarabanda sometimes played, and Peter Pye did a few sessions there too. Sometimes I wasn't sure who would turn up to play, but the overall sound was always good because of the great acoustics of the place. There were perks to the job too - free food and free drinks all night long! I used to drive there and drive back home again in the early hours, and after drinking Heineken beer for most of the evening I must have been pretty drunk. It's just as well that there were no breathalysers or drink driving regulations in those days. I did this job for around two years before Pizza Hut realised that the venue, because of its location, would always be full of paying customers whether there was live music or not. After the job finished, Pizza Hut did not continue their experiment with live music, but Pizza Express had noticed the success of the venture and started to successfully include live jazz in some of their own restaurants.

GROWING

'No rain means no rainbow'

I had become tired of trying to succeed in the music business. Although I had had what some may call a very successful time, playing, touring, writing and recording, I did not FEEL successful. I still felt like Joe Bloggs and knew there was a niche in the world for me that I had not yet found. In that sense, the offers of display work from Warner Bros and a couple of other smaller record companies, came at a very interesting time. It was strangely Ironic that I had tried for so long to obtain a recording contract for Zarabanda with one of the major record companies and now here they were, banging on my door and begging for my services.

I was interviewed for the job with Warner Bros at their offices at Alperton, West London. I was given a very welcoming and friendly kind of interview by a couple of the managers and felt as though the job was in my pocket without very much effort on my part. I started a couple of weeks later and was pleasantly surprised by the amount of money that I was to earn and the various perks that I would receive. A nice new estate car, parking, petrol, tax and insurance all paid; telephone and all communication expenses paid; a daily lunch allowance, plus hotels or any other expenses deemed necessary to do the job.

During this job and the time that I previously worked as a freelancer for record companies, I saw just how corrupt the business was. Things went on that were innocently called 'sales and marketing' but in my eyes I saw corruption and bribery.

The record charts were an integral and important part of record manufacture, business and retailing, and to get a record in the charts was the aim of most record companies and recording artists. The record charts were created from the sales of an elite group of record shops, known in the business as 'chart shops'. My first experience of how shops reported their sales, which made up the 'Pop Charts', was purely accidental. I bumped into a record company rep that I knew who was in the office of a record shop with the shop manager. He was instructing just what records should be included in the shops 'diary' - the weekly return of record sales. These diaries were used to compile the 'charts.' He was obviously trying to 'fix' the position of the company's records in the chart. He winked at me and I pretended to ignore the business that was going on. He was one of many all over the UK, visiting shops and controlling imaginary sales that were recorded in order to compile the charts.

The sales 'diaries' eventually disappeared and an electronic system of recording sales was introduced. Each chart shop had an electronic machine, which would be remotely accessed at midnight every Friday by an automatic telephone line that recorded the record shops total sales for the week. The record numbers would be entered manually into the machine during the week as each sale was made. Record companies got around this by supplying the retailer with a list of their 'priorities'

- five or six important records that had to show 'sales' and *had* to climb the charts. It was, however, obvious to the authorities that record sales were still being manipulated by the record companies and so a new 'foolproof' way of recording legitimate sales was introduced. Bar codes were included on the covers of every album and single, and in order to record the sale, every record had to be scanned by the scanner always positioned close to the till. Not to be beaten, the record companies supplied each rep with a set of dummy bar codes for their six 'priorities'. Each week, the new set of bar codes was placed near the till where the retailer could easily scan the codes without directly incriminating the representative. Some of these dummy bar codes remained the same for a period of weeks if the record company was determined for a top ten position, other less important records only remained for a week or so. The record shops were encouraged to keep manipulating the charts by scanning these priority (dummy) bar codes when the shop was empty and no sale had actually been made. Gifts (bribes) from the reps of free records, picture disks and 'white labels' assisted greatly with this activity. Limited edition picture discs and 'advance copies' were given out which were worth a lot more than the face value of a normal single or album. If the priority record or album did not climb the charts, the reps would be in the following week asking the dealer "What happened?" The scam was repeated every week in hundreds of chart shops throughout the length and breadth of Great Britain. All of the record companies took part and each one had their own unique way of helping to create the Top Ten and The Top Twenty, which was used as the basis for radio and TV music programmes, whilst of course bringing in the profits for the record companies.

I found my own display work at Warner Bros quite easy, although there were large areas of England to be covered during one single day. I could have stayed away in a hotel as any hotel expenses were met without question, but I felt better always getting the work done and getting back home. I have never really liked hotels. As I became more involved with the company and the job, my skills were required on a regular basis in London's West End. My displays became bigger, bolder and more artistic and original. Any Warner artists touring, would have to have their products displayed in the major West End stores, as it was important for foreign management to see that their artistes were being supported and promoted well in London. Harrods and Selfridges record departments, HMV, Virgin, Tower Records and Our Price (all now closed), had to be convinced by me that it was in their interest to give some big advertising space in their stores to the latest album of an artist that was touring or visiting the country from the USA.

I also had to cover the new album launches where the artist would attend together with a large entourage, in order to promote their new album to a large group of journalists and media types who were wined and dined with no expense spared. Some of these media types were so fat, I am sure they made a career out of traveling around on a daily basis to various record launches and promotional events - just for the food!

Whilst I was working at Warner Bros, we broke many new acts successfully; Madonna, Simply Red, Prince, ZZ Top, REM, Enya and many others all had their record launches (and lunches) in London. Rod Stewart, Foreigner and Fleetwood Mac also had hit records, courtesy of the efforts of everyone at Warners. It was an eye opener to see how the other half lived and worked, and from always being on stage in front of audiences I saw how the other business side of music operated. It certainly was a shock for me to see that people working in the record companies actually knew very little about music, but often came from diverse sales orientated backgrounds. Most of them couldn't even recognise the beat of a song and tap their foot in time with it if they tried; I always noticed that they were not tapping in time with the record. If they were told by the managing director that something was good, they would like it, even though it might be rubbish. The managing Director once stood on a stage in front of hundreds of international delegates, promising that the artist he had just signed in London would in twelve months' time be the biggest artist in the world. The subsequent records flopped, I can't even remember the name of the artist. The promise and the records were conveniently forgotten. There was a lot of hype when the sales force were convinced by the management that something was good. I often had to bite my lip when some of this music was presented to the sales force, and I wondered how on earth some of these awful records were made and released, when Zarabanda had found the process so difficult.

The company often looked to smaller record labels for musical talent. The smaller label and its roster of artists would be purchased or contracted and then digested into the larger company. 'Everything but the girl' and 'Simply Red' were both picked up by Warners using this method, most of the other real talent came from the USA or from established UK acts such as Rod Stewart or Fleetwood Mac.

Five years had passed since I began taking karate classes, and I had subsequently passed my Black Belt grading after failing it the first time. For me, the Black Belt was an incentive to work and train even harder to learn and improve. In 1984 I had a small operation on my left leg which put me out of action for some time and frustrated my efforts to improve. I tried to get back to training too soon and made the leg even worse and my recovery even slower. I started practising on my own at Waltham Forest College (Chingford Annexe), close to one of the record shops that I used to visit, in order to regain my technique and speed. This small venue was to become my own very first Karate Club.

There were always one or two people who watched me making efforts to rehabilitate myself in this tiny venue and in 1985 when my leg had finally recovered, I advertised for members of the new Chingford Karate Club. I considered that if I had to stand in front of people and teach them the basics of Karate, then my own technique would have to return and of course improve. One of the first to enrol at the new Chingford Karate Club was Chris Lafbury who I am very pleased to say, is still with me thirty five years later. There were no other Karate clubs at that time and there was a lot of hesitancy from the council and schools to give permission for me to start one up. The school halls were controlled by the local council, and as Waltham Forest council did not allow Karate classes in any of their schools or halls, the college was an ideal location, as it was outside of the direct jurisdiction of the local council. The classes at Waltham Forest College continued during the non-Summer months and were held in what was affectionately known as the Judo bay (or sweat box). It was a small concrete room much like a prison cell, around ten meters square with no windows and no heating. If the weather was hot outside the students would lose pounds in sweat, but if it was cold, it took me ages to get the class warmed up and active. As the weeks went on, I found that the class was growing larger as more and more people signed up and started my Karate classes. I allowed children to start in the class, but at the time I considered that to be a big mistake. The children were quite troublesome and being relatively inexperienced, I had not quite developed the skills to deal with them. During the class one evening, one young lad looked very uncomfortable. I ignored his rather pained expression thinking he just didn't like doing karate. As I brought the class back to the relaxed and informal position, I noticed a pool of fluid on the floor around the feet of the young lad. His trousers were soaked through, and even with my limited knowledge, it was obvious that he had weed himself. I went up to him and quietly suggested that he should go to the toilet.

"I don't want to go" came the reply and so I repeated the request a little more sternly.

"I don't want to go" said the boy again. I then said "I really think you should go to the toilet, look at all that wee on the floor!" Without blinking he looked up at me and said –

"It wasn't me."

The whole class erupted in laughter at the poor lad's misfortune, his denial and misplaced comments. I should add at this point that some children were forced to come to the classes by parents who considered that they needed their children to have discipline, respect and concentration instilled into them. These children left the weekly classes in shock after enduring an hour of almost military discipline, something they had rarely experienced in life before Karate. The parents loved it, the children hated it! Some children thrived on the discipline and actually enjoyed it; these were the ones who excelled and did well, passing gradings with distinction and doing well in competitions.

As the college venue was closed during exam, time I tried desperately to get the council to allow me to use a school hall for classes. It was like talking to a brick wall. Whoever I spoke to just brushed my requests aside or were not available for me to see. The education department, which was responsible for school lettings in those days, never returned my calls, and when I did get through, the staff were always out or 'in a meeting'. The Mayor of Waltham Forest became involved and I soon found myself with some important friends who supported the idea of a school Karate Club in the area. John Baker, one of the club's senior grades, worked for the council and he helped considerably in getting karate accepted by the education department. After finally breaking down the barriers of prejudice against karate, the council relented and I was able to try out virtually all of the schools in the Chingford area, finally settling in Rushcroft School which had the most wonderful pine clad gymnasium, perfect for a Karate Dojo.

I found that I had the ability to teach and make the classes interesting and fun for the adults and children who took part in the lessons. I had to make sure that my days of display work finished with enough time for me to get to the club and take the classes. I realised that Karate was taking precedence over everything else, including my job at Warner Bros, and even my life long ambitions in music. This was actually quite a good thing, as I was easily drawn to the drugs that went along with the music business (I enjoyed that side of life probably more than I should have done). With the emphasis now firmly on Karate, I regularly took part in the two-week special Karate courses during May and September, hosted by Sensei Enoeda and held at Crystal Palace National Sports Centre, and I had to make sure that dates for work, family and Karate courses did not clash.

Whilst doing the job at Warner Bros., I still did a bit of playing and performing in the evenings or at weekends. My friend, Billy Ritchie, had persuaded me that I should go out as a one man band. I had the amplifiers and the equipment and got hold of a rhythm box (a kind of electronic drum machine). I used echo to enhance my rather suspect voice, and with the PA and the drum machine, created a reasonably acceptable sound. The money for doing these type of shows was very good and the venues were generally rather rough pubs, where most musicians with brains feared to play. Knife fights and even gun crime were quite common in these kind of locations, and quite often some of the audience would be drunk or fighting before you even started the music.

There was a gang fight in one of my regular venues - 'The Orange Tree' at Friern Barnet. Billiard cues were being used as weapons and around a dozen youths were involved in the bar fight. The situation became even more violent, and the pub boss - a very large Irishman - waded in and started throwing some of the trouble makers out. When it got to the point that he was getting beaten up, I stopped playing and put my guitar down to go and give him a hand. He turned around to me and shouted "Don't stop the focking (sic) music - keep playing" - whilst he banged the heads together of the last three or four trouble makers and threw them out. He brushed himself down, wiped the blood from his face and returned to the bar whilst reprimanding me for stopping the music because of the fight. He was a large tough Irishman, and the following week he was found stabbed to death on the floor of the toilet in 'The Orange Tree'.

I did this kind of work for a while, but one evening after arriving at a pub in Caledonian Rd. to do a show, I found one of the punters drunk on the floor outside the pub door. I put my equipment back in the car and drove home. I had had enough. I then rang the agent and told him to 'stick it'.

It wasn't really necessary to do this kind of playing now that I had the job at Warners. The money was coming in and so I felt happy to stop playing in such dodgy places. I investigated moving to a larger house while things were looking good (and perhaps before the company I worked for went bust and I lost my job again).

ANOTHER BOMB

'Grief is the price we pay for love'
The Queen

M y family moved to our new and larger house - 8 Rowantree Rd in a select part of Winchmore Hill in North London. I had done just about every improvement to our previous home at 28 Dimsdale Drive in Enfield and was glad that this new house was beautifully decorated and in very good condition. I certainly did not want to start knocking walls down and redecorating everything once again. The price was high because of its condition and the work that had been done, but although a wonderful home, this new address did not bring a wonderful life to my family. There seemed to be more quarrels disputes and arguments and I think we were all happier in the previous smaller house which was cosy and more like a real home. I seemed to be working harder and harder, and with the pressures of my job and together with my efforts to improve in Karate, I was rarely home. This in itself created more problems; I was not being a full time Father and not being a proper husband. Things seemed to be going wrong, but neither my wife Rita or myself seemed to have the ability or the incentive to put things right. The house reflected this, becoming tatty, unrepaired, untidy and dirty.

The latent problems in the relationship between my wife and my Mum surfaced a few years earlier in a very unfortunate manner. I encouraged Rita to take some time out and take baby Daren for a break in Devon to spend a bit of time with my Mum. I thought that this would be a good chance for them both to clear the air and get to know each other a little better. It didn't work. There was an awful argument while they were together and the rift became irreparable, my Mother never visiting our home again. On my Mother's rare visits to London, I would pick her up from Paddington Station, we would have a light lunch together and I would take her over to her very good friend Peggy Pye (Peter Pye's Mother), where she would stay for a week or so. During her stays I would go over and spend some time with her, taking her out for the day or going out for a meal together. It was sad that she was never made welcome again at the family home, but I believe the situation had reached stalemate.

It was on one of these visits that I thought it would be nice to drive her past our old house at 7 Millais Rd. in Bush Hill Park. Cars were parked tightly along both sides of the narrow road and so I drove slowly, coming almost to a stop in the middle of the road outside our old home. At that point the front door of our house opened and a gentleman came out. He saw the car which had now stopped and wondered what my mother was doing staring at him in what must have appeared to be a rather rude and strange manner. My Mother suddenly opened the car door and jumped out. 'Oh no' I thought (and then said), and I also jumped out hoping to reassure the man that he was not about to be attacked or robbed. My Mother was already in the front garden pointing and looking incredulous at her pink and blue hydrangeas which were still alive, blooming and doing well. I reassured the man - the present occupant of the home, that we were not insane, we were visiting the area and used to live at the address years previously. He became excited. He started talking loudly in Italian and called to his family inside. Other members of his family came to the front door and he explained to them that we used to live in the house. That was it. We were both invited into the house and had to meet the parents, the grandparents and all of the children who were living there together. They were all lined up in the kitchen and we had to be greeted by each family member and exchange kisses, handshakes and greetings in Italian. The man kindly showed us the back garden (with the 'lean to' still intact). We saw my Mother's flowering cherry tree covered in bright pink blossom and we explained just how small the tree was when we planted it many years previously. Mrs Gabriel, our neighbour from next door, was rushed in and there were tears of excitement and happiness all round. Everyone started crying, including the Italian family. It was a touching and happy reunion with our old house, and I was of course pleased that I had decided to make that small trip down memory lane, giving us all such a surprising and memorable time.

When my Mother was living in Devon, I never missed sending her flowers for her Birthday or Mother's day, however, it was a sad and unfortunate situation and the flowers probably did little to ease the pain of everything that had gone on. Occasionally our families would meet up at my Sister Jan's home in Torquay for Christmas or special occasions. I found the tension very difficult to resolve and even understand. Suffice to say that my own family never really got on with my Mum and Jan's family, there were some nice times, but these times were always overshadowed by an invisible cloak of suspicion and innuendo - a look or a nod, a sigh or a retreat to the bedroom or toilet. I wanted so much for everyone to get on together, but it did not happen.

Mum passed away in 1988. I got the phone message that she was sick and had been taken to hospital while I was teaching Karate at the club. The following morning I took the train down to Torquay. When I asked to see her, the little Irish nurse told me that she was just having a wash, and so I thought that she must be feeling better. Then someone else who could see that I hadn't understood the message, told me that she had passed away. I laughed and cried at the same time with the ridiculous irony of the situation. I always consider that this is my Mum's joke; a way of making me smile even now after all of these years. I cried at the time, but now I smile every time I think of it.

I was not ready for losing her. I always considered somewhat childishly, that she would go on forever and always be there. It was like having the umbilical cord cut once again, but this time there would be no happy ending, no smiles, no 'happy ever after'. I took the pain very deeply and still feel it years later, together with the guilt that always accompanies loss.

❋ ❋ ❋

Jan and I arranged the funeral in a beautiful little church set in the countryside of Devon, the one that hosted the funeral of her own Brother Clarence a few years earlier. The sun shone brightly through the coloured stained glass windows as we looked skyward and we sang one of Mum's favourite hymns - 'God be in my head'. We brought her ashes back to London to be buried with my Dad in Edmonton Cemetery. There were just a few of us there for the small sad ceremony, but I was pleased that Mum's long time friend, Peggy Pye, was there with us. All of these years later I still think about her most days. Things she said pop into my mind, together with the advice she distributed in such a regular and serious way. I have never got over losing her but I suppose I have got used to her not actually being there. It's silly things like going into a card shop and seeing personalised cards for 'Mum' or 'Mothers Day', I still find that difficult even after all these years.

I would have liked to learn more about my Father, Alfred Albert Butler or 'Alf' to my Mother. I know that he grew up in Tottenham in quite a poor family. We knew about his Mother but knew little about his Father, who seemed to have disappeared without trace. Word was, he was killed in a horse-riding accident, but there seems little actual evidence of this. After searching a map, I found my Father's home address in Tottenham had now been replaced by a block of flats. I would like to have seen his early home and known more about him.

After my Mother's death I decided to visit one of her brothers, Percy, who still lived in Bedford. He was only too pleased to talk to me about my Mothers early life and he kindly took me to see the previous family homes. I could see quite easily that my Mother's side of the family was different to my Fathers. The family seemed quite well off, living in a nice part of Bedford. Rooms in the family's large house were often rented to teachers and travellers who were in the area. I imagine that this is how my Mother and Father first met; him as a travelling representative staying the house, and her, a young woman going about her daily household chores. The family also had a small dairy shop on a corner in the centre of Bedford, which produced ice cream, butter and milk for the locals. Being the only daughter with seven brothers in those days, meant a lot of hard work for a young girl who, as well as regularly having to clean all of her brother's shoes, had to help out in the dairy and assist with the general household chores. This indoctrinated habit of hard work followed my Mother throughout her life and formed a large part of who she actually was.

As the Rayner family gradually married and dispersed, it became clear that the financial legacy created from the property and the dairy, had all but disappeared, slowly whittled away by the Mother's drinking habit. For many years she drank heavily on a daily basis in a high street pub, whilst her youngest children, including my Mother, sat outside waiting for her to finish drinking. My uncle Percy explained this to me and he showed me the pub (now an off licence) in the High St of Bedford. He also showed me the various Rayner homes which the family moved to throughout the pre-war years, as finances became increasingly tighter. I discovered most of this rather sobering, but interesting family history as an adult, years after the end of the War.

On this visit to try to retrace some of my Mothers earlier life, we visited the childhood and lifelong friend of my Mother who was still alive and still living in Bedford. Her home looked like a kind of 'grace and favour' home, given to those who are very old and in need of support. We entered reverently due to the quiet nature of the home, there was a kind of dark peacefulness that I had only ever felt before in a Church when services were over.

As my eyes became accustomed to the lack of light, I could see table lamps glowing with their light barely penetrating the thick brown lampshades with tassels hanging from their edges, although it was still daylight outside. Thick black frames housed pictures hanging on the walls and the furniture was black and very ornate, unlike anything I had ever seen before. At a time somewhere in the future I would be tempted to imagine that this is what it would be like to visit a home during the reign of Queen Victoria. Daylight could barely be seen through the thick lace curtains hanging at the windows of the French doors, but I could see the lady was very old, sitting down, speaking quietly and looking much older than my mother when I last saw her. Memories of my Mother were spoken, quietly and respectfully; the friendships and the dancing in a local hall on Friday nights. We felt like intruders and left the kindly old lady after a short while, I, feeling as though I had visited a different age as I stumbled out into the daylight.

My mother as a child on the left with her baby brother and her Mother on the right

PARTING OF
THE WAYS

'More Power to Your Elbow' – My Mum

1988 proved to be a time of great change in many ways. As well as the shock of my Mother's death, there were to be changes with my Karate Clubs and later on changes in my job.

* * *

I enjoyed the fun whilst working at Warner Bros. There were regular sales meetings which included some great food and drinks. Annual conferences were always enjoyable, with staff coming from all over the UK and Europe, to the music conferences which included presentations from the label managers of all the new records that were to be released. Sometimes these conferences were held in England but one of the best was held in Switzerland, with lots of parties and visits to some live music clubs. I always had to arrive at these events a few days earlier than everyone else in order to produce and install displays of posters and record sleeves featuring all the acts that were signed to the company. Another really good conference was held in Ireland where we all sampled the greatest ever seafood with the most generous measures of vodka, whiskey or rum that I had ever seen, plus of course the ever famous Irish Guinness.

There were always some boyish pranks at these record company events, with people getting thrown into swimming pools, or luggage that had suspiciously disappeared. These things were generally accepted by the management as part of our corporate bonding, which would ultimately help with the company sales figures and its young hip profile. One of the best pranks involved me, although I had nothing whatsoever to do in implementing it. In the hotels we always shared rooms - usually two per room. I was billeted with a new lad, a young and keen salesman. All of our luggage and clothing had been unpacked and tidied away in our room and the evening was free for us to generally enjoy ourselves with a few drinks. We both returned to the room worse for wear in the early hours of the morning and unlocked the hotel door. The room was empty; no beds, no cupboards, no luggage or any item of furniture. We considered that we must have the wrong room and went trying all of the doors nearby that looked like ours. The key did not fit any of the doors and the occupants sounded pretty fed up with being disturbed by a couple of drunks. After searching unsuccessfully for our room and belongings we decided to sleep on the floor of the empty room. We just lay down on the floor in our clothes to try to get a couple of hours sleep. In the morning we discovered that we were the victims of a prank. All of the furniture including the beds and cupboards had been removed from the room and put in the lifts! No one could use the lifts and we had to call reception to find someone available to return all of the room's furniture. All of our inebriated searching and frustration the previous night had been watched and enjoyed by the hidden and giggling team of perpetrators. I thought it was a great wheeze and it was certainly a good initiation for the new salesman.

The National Accounts Manager was also on the receiving end of one of these pranks. He was a young and very smart man, very successful in the job that he did, envied by the sales men and swooned over by most of the girls in the company. Good looking and dressed in his Armani suit and Rolex watch, he was picked up by the sales guys and thrown into the deep end of the hotel swimming pool where one of the conferences was being held. Nobody bothered to find out if he could swim or not, but he managed to pull himself out of the pool, swearing and cursing us all. We all enjoyed the spectacle of seeing him in his posh suit, dripping wet and cursing, as he never normally had a hair out of place and always looked immaculate.

One of the benefits of working for the company was access to free concert tickets. We were encouraged with these tickets to go along to concerts performed in London in order to support the acts concerned and show commitment as a record company team. Many of these shows were awful, but we did get to see some very good acts; Prince, Madonna, Rod Stewart and quite a few others were usually well oversubscribed, as the demand for tickets from staff was great. At this time I received a request from a friend of mine; Jeff Skinner, was a Frank Sinatra fan and when a series of Sinatra concerts at the Albert Hall became sold out, he begged me to try to obtain tickets. He didn't mind paying and so I went to the label manager's office and asked if any tickets were available.

"I'll try but I think all seats have been sold, come back and see me next week" came the reply.

I went back the following week and asked casually if there was any news of tickets for the Frank Sinatra show.

"Well, I haven't got tickets but think I can get you into see the concert. You have to go to the stage door at 7.00 pm on Saturday, ask for Dave, tell him your name and the two of you should get in OK, that's the best I can do I am afraid."

I was not really a Frank Sinatra fan and I didn't originally envisage going along with my friend in order to get him in. However I thanked the label manager for his trouble and reported the news back to my friend Jeff.

I explained the rather odd situation and told him that I doubted that we would actually get in to see the show but that it maybe just worth a try. I considered that I had been given a very polite 'no' answer from the label manager, disguised as an unlikely pass through the stage door of the Albert Hall with a possibility of maybe just standing in the balcony. We decided to give it a try and got suitably dressed up for the occasion - or maybe the non-occasion. As instructed, we arrived at the stage door and asked for Dave. I was more surprised than Jeff when we were actually ushered in through the stage door. We were told to wait in the corridor where we were shortly met by a very smart and efficient chap who requested us to follow him around corridors and down some stairs then into a small private bar. We were left there alone and ordered a couple of drinks. Our money was waved away and we smiled as we downed a few free vodkas. After a short while, more people arrived in the bar - very well dressed and with an obvious air of celebrity. The small bar became quite full with maybe twenty or so semi-familiar faces. At that point *Frank Sinatra* walked into the bar with a couple of others. Jeff nearly fainted and I spilt my drink. Frank Sinatra proceeded to walk round and be introduced to everyone present, shaking hands and making small talk. Both Jeff and I were shaking - myself with fear and Jeff with excitement. He was making his way around the bar - just one or two people away from us; he was smiling, laughing and mesmerising everyone in that room with his brilliant blue eyes and his personality.

"Well, I gotta go now, I've got a show to do." He smiled and left.

It was probably a wonderful stroke of fate that he nipped out of the bar before we got introduced - I would have probably ruined the record company's future with one of it's most celebrated artistes. The bar quickly emptied and Jeff and I were left looking at each other and wondering if we would actually get to see the show. The smart and efficient chap who first took us into the bar, beckoned again for us to follow him. Around some more corridors, down some more stairs and into the main arena with two seats just inches from the front of the stage! Roger Moore was just a few seats away and as we were both busy 'celebrity spotting' the show began. There he was in all of his glory, the big band swinging and hit after hit being delivered flawlessly. I was converted. Sinatra was something else. I could now see what all the fuss was about and I could see just why he was such a tremendous star worldwide. We had a fantastic night and went out for a great meal after the show.

The following week I went back to the office in

Kensington to thank the label manager for his efforts in getting us in to see the show.

"Oh, did you get in then? I really didn't think you would."

There is a moral there somewhere, I'm not sure what it is though.

Nobody wanted to admit it but the writing was on the wall and we blindly welcomed it with open arms; the CD had arrived. One of my jobs was to introduce the CD to the public who were very suspicious of something that looked nothing like a 12' vinyl album. There was a great reluctance from the public in accepting the CD in a commercial sense, and so I pinned dummy CDs on to my normal album displays in order to educate the public and let them be aware that the album displayed was available in vinyl and CD format. I was unknowingly banging nails into the coffin of the vinyl LP and my own job. Classical music adopted the CD earlier and much quicker than other forms of music, then jazz and then the back catalogue of the record companies. It soon became a race to see which companies could offer the most titles in CD format, and within a year or so the whole record industry had changed, with the CD as the new format for buying music. The record companies made a fortune at this time as the back catalogue music they already had on tape cost just pennies to reproduce on a CD, which was then sold on to the public at a hugely inflated price. The public's appetite for the CD grew fast, as collections of vinyl were replaced with CDs costing around £8, £10 or £12. Vinyl records were soon dropped from mainstream production and record companies geared up to producing 99% CDs. Shops changed too. There were no more big window or in-store displays; shops were just filled with racks and racks of CDs. That is the point where I read and understood the writing on the wall. There was turmoil at Warner Bros. as warehouse and dispatch staff were sacked and contracts with vinyl producers were torn up. The company's big storage and dispatch depot at Alperton was not needed any more and I got out at that point. I was the last display merchandiser to leave the company.

It was a shock having to pay for my car, petrol and telephone plus all of the other luxuries that I had become used to, although I didn't actually have any real or pressing financial worries. I had always saved, and my Mum's favourite saying 'Money is your best friend' had been instilled into me from a very early age. I had paid off most of the mortgage on the house while I was earning good money from the job and playing the music. I was also renting out a small flat that I had bought and was paying for with a mortgage, the rent from this also brought in a few extra pounds. There was a small and steady income from teaching at the Karate clubs and so I decided to try to grow the clubs and increase my income from this source. I had been self-employed before, and at this point in time I had had enough of working for companies that all seemed to go down the pan.

MORE KARATE

'There is no first attack in Karate' - Gichin Funakoshi

I was becoming addicted to Karate, and felt that I had to train every day in order to improve. I felt compelled to move forward with the club and with my own training, and so in 1988 resigned from the karate organisation I was with, feeling that there were restraints that were holding me back. I started a second club at Wanstead Leisure Centre and joined the famous Marshall St Dojo of the legendary Sensei Enoeda, doing my training three days a week during my lunchtimes, whilst working in the West End for Warner Bros. These classes were high intensity and very physical. I did three classes during lunchtimes every Monday, Wednesday and Friday; a beginners' class, an intermediate class and a Black Belt class. I would rush back to my West End job after these Karate classes, get the work finished, drive home, have my evening meal and rush off to take classes in my own club based in Chingford and now my second club in Wanstead. I was learning, improving and earning a good living, but understandably of course, family life suffered.

I was often being asked to assist with teaching duties at Sensei Enoeda's dojo in London's West End. This was a responsibility which I took seriously and did to the best of my ability. I was honoured to do these sessions, as the dojo was an important Mecca for students from across the world to visit. Sensei Enoeda was revered as a kind of Karate God, and the main reason students came from abroad was to have sight of Sensei Enoeda and the Marshall St dojo and maybe take part in one of his sessions. If Sensei Enoeda was away when these visitors arrived, they still wanted to train in the Enoeda dojo and have their picture taken at the end of the class. Sometimes, whilst teaching for Sensei Enoeda, a student would arrive, get changed and peer around the door that led into the dojo. Seeing that Sensei Enoeda was not present, the student would head off back to the changing room, get changed and leave. This didn't happen often, but it did give an indication of a student's strange attitude to training. On the other side of the coin, there would often be senior instructors, higher grades than myself, who would arrive for training, get into line and train hard regardless of who was teaching. When teaching, I was often a lower grade than these Black Belts, but against any respectful protests that I made to a senior grade, I still had to carry on and deliver the karate classes that Sensei Enoeda expected.

I found that I got to know and see more of Sensei Enoeda and how he worked in the dojo and behind the scenes in the office and at home. I was voted on to the committee for the club and helped with the general administration. I was asked to write Sensei Enoeda's speeches for his Christmas parties, and became the chairman of his Marshall St committee. He always gave a speech at the annual Christmas party and always finished the speech off by singing with a strong Japanese accent, one of the old standards. Speeches had to be written out in advance so that he could practice the pronunciation. I had to be careful not to include too many 'Ls' or 'Rs' in the speech text, because of the difficulty that the Japanese have with pronouncing these letters. I always smiled secretly to myself on courses when at the end of the session, Sensei Enoeda would raise his arms into the air for 'deep breeding' (deep breathing). On one occasion I asked him about the books he had written and the absence of the fourth volume in his incomplete set of three Karate Kata books; 'Bruddy Pubrishers' came the gruff reply, and there was little more to be said. I worked hard for Sensei Enoeda and the Marshall St dojo but enjoyed every minute of it, not realising that it would all come to a swift, unplanned and sudden stop in the not too distant future.

1987, on a course with Sensei Enoeda.

Everything seemed to be going well and I felt humbled by much of my responsibility and success. In 1992 Capital Radio offered a prize trip to Japan with spending money and all expenses paid and I decided to take part in the competition and try to win the prize.

Each day on the radio a question about Japan was broadcast, so that at the end of the week the five answers to the daily questions had to be sent by postcard to Capital Radio. The winner would be picked from the pile of correct answers on the following Monday. Of course, on Monday I was at home listening intently to the radio whilst my wife Rita, Daren and Simone laughed at me and mocked me for expecting to be the winner. The tension mounted as we all huddled around the radio listening for the announcement of the winner. I held my breath as the winning card was plucked from the pile. And the winner is.................Rod Butler! My family stood open mouthed in shock, the phone rang and there I was - live on Capital Radio. I explained my interest in Karate and Japanese culture and tried hard to give a sensible interview as we were broadcasting live on the air. The trip was a great success and enabled me to train regularly at the JKA dojo in Tokyo with many of the instructors that I had trained under during the Crystal Palace courses in London. I also travelled to Kyoto to see some of the ancient history of Japan and visit the National Martial Arts Centre. I visited the dojo of the late Master Masatoshi Nakayama - The Hoitsukan, which was kept open by his wife and supported by his students and visitors. The students of the Chingford and Wanstead clubs all gained from my experiences in Japan when I finally returned home to England.

It was at this point in 1992 that I strayed from the marital path. At the Wanstead club, a new group of beginners arrived to enrol and the attraction to one young lady was immediate and mutual. I had been hit on the head with a very large mallet and I was seeing stars. They say that love is a kind of madness and it certainly was. I lost all of the normal skills of common sense and judgement and went headlong into a relationship with a young lady barely 21 years old. Suddenly I was 15 again and crazy, doing things that were not considered acceptable for a man in his 40s. It seemed as if I was on a runaway train unable to stop at any station and unable to even pause for breath.

The relationship lasted for around two years. It was explosively volatile and I had difficulty in maintaining any sort of equilibrium during this time. I decided that I knew little at all about the female of the species and felt as if there was a whole section of my own social education that was missing. I left home and moved into the flat that I had been renting out. This gave me some space to try to understand what was happening to me. Up to this point my extra-marital relationship was totally platonic.

After a few false endings the relationship came to an end. I needed time and space to recover from the hurricane that I had just gone through. I wanted to reassess my life, my work and my future. I rested and took refuge again in the Karate that I loved. I did the male menopause thing and bought a sports car - a light blue Toyota MR2. I sought the company of females, not for any sort of relationship, but to just talk and try to put into place the missing parts of my understanding about females and how relationships work. From a very young age, I found normal interaction with the opposite sex difficult to deal with, and the problems I encountered usually traced their way back to my early childhood years. The embarrassment and particularly the shyness I felt, meant that from a young age normal relationships evaded me. I felt battered and insecure; I needed to talk and got myself into counselling. I found a lady counsellor who helped me fit all the pieces of the jigsaw together. I used to go in to these counselling meetings not knowing what to talk about, but came out an hour later feeling as if a great weight had been lifted from my shoulders. I could look up at the blue sky again and smile. Happy. Of course these meetings did not actually change anything but they did help me view lots of things from a different perspective. It was naturally difficult to begin talking about very personal thoughts and feelings that I had, but I found that once the trust had been created, I could talk about anything and everything with total freedom and honesty. The experience was totally liberating and I continued with these meetings for over a year.

I subsequently found that I enjoyed the freedom of being on my own. After coming out of a marriage and then a stressful two year relationship, I did not have and did not want or need a relationship with the opposite sex; I did not want a relationship at all.

There is always a price to be paid for a broken marriage; a debt that is never truly settled or paid off. With some there are financial problems, home problems, or possibly custody of the young children to be fought over. Whatever the compensation or retribution, it is never enough to the injured party. In my own case I was viewed (probably quite rightly) as the perpetrator of the 'crime' and my family of son and daughter became more distant. My punishment meant that I would never be able to enjoy those dreamt of days in the sun with everyone happy together. Somehow I secretly imagine that this ambition or dream would never have been realised, even if the marriage had stayed in tact.

My daughter, Simone, had moved in with me at the flat for a while to concentrate and work on her 'A' level exams. She had her own 'demons' to face, and I wanted to support her in her endeavours. I gave her the run of the place to lay out work on the floor in order to study with no interruptions. I concentrated on my Karate and she concentrated on her studies.

I trained harder and studied the details of the basic Karate techniques and Kata on a deeper level. I pushed myself harder and further during my own training in the classes at Marshall St. and found that Karate challenged me on a physical, spiritual and intellectual level. If Sensei Enoeda was in the dojo, there would be three consecutive classes for me to take part in and I knew that I would be finding my own weaknesses, challenging and re-defining the limits of my own Karate skills. As well as the advanced classes, I always took part in the first white belt class which included total beginners and a few students who like myself wanted to understand the deeper essence of Karate. The second class was primarily for intermediate students who had been training for maybe a year or two, and the third class was for Black and Brown Belts, many of whom had been studying Karate for ten, twenty or thirty years. I would always encourage Black Belts who wish to improve, to attend beginners classes in order to understand further the techniques they perform.

One day I arrived a little late for the first class. I got changed into my Gi and decided, as I was late and out of respect, I would not enter the class. The class was quiet, not the usual expected Martial noise. When approaching the dojo entrance I saw Sensei Enoeda teaching just one student; he was the only one who had arrived for that first beginners class. Later on I wondered if this lucky student had continued with his karate studies and if he realised how fortunate he was having a one to one personal lesson with Sensei Enoeda.

Apart from the normal classes with Sensei Enoeda and the advanced classes at Crystal Palace, one of the greatest Karate classes I ever took part in was a beginners white belt class at Marshall St, again when Sensei Enoeda was teaching. I arrived early for the class, got changed and joined a small number of students in the dojo waiting for the class to begin. After a short warm up we were taken through all of the basic single techniques that form the foundations that all Karate progress is built upon. We then did the formal three step sparring a couple of times and finished off with 'Kihon Kata', the most rudimentary of all Shotokan Kata. Everything was performed at full speed and with full power, and after just thirty minutes we had all given just about everything we physically had to this class. I seemed to go through and past the tiredness, the breathlessness and the weakness that always pervades such a basic class. I became as light as air and felt as though I could go on forever. I felt as though anything was possible and I didn't want that class to end. Eventually I staggered dripping wet with sweat, out of the dojo, my mind illuminated to the possibilities of Karate. It was a fantastic class and although very basic, it seemed to summarise for me, everything that Karate was. There have been a few of these classes where I have found a new higher level of consciousness, becoming much lighter, stronger and faster than normal. These times are unplanned and unpredictable and usually occur when I have reached the state of total exhaustion but just continue on, oblivious to the tiredness. Something seems to 'switch on', but I don't know what that switch is, or how it is operated.

Sometimes during a class, Sensei Enoeda would stand close and shout, demanding that your technique be faster or your kicks higher. From somewhere, the strength came to fulfil all of his demands, and he would respond with a booming '*Yes*'. Sometimes I thought he was standing behind me in the class and my attacking and defending power would be increased dramatically. I sensed his presence but he was not there, he was in a different position entirely. Wherever he was during the class, he seemed to have a tremendous effect on all of the students.

I started working harder at building on the success of my own clubs and visitors started appearing from abroad to come and train with us either at Chingford or Wanstead. I began to be even more involved with Sensei Enoeda's Marshall St dojo, teaching and generally assisting with administration. Sensei Enoeda began preliminary work on a series of videos and books, and I was 'volunteered' to assist him with these projects. I was asked to film some of the rehearsals with my video camera and take some photos with my Nikon. I viewed all of this as a way to enhance my own knowledge and skill in order to improve and learn more. I was surprised at the vast variation in techniques and realised that there is no 'one true' way of performing a technique in a kata; people have different sized limbs, different opinions and different applications of techniques, and so there are naturally some variations. I saw this on a few occasions during rehearsals when Sensei Enoeda referred to books and made international telephone calls to ascertain certain technical details and variations within a kata before I filmed him.

My own clubs went from strength to strength,

and I started to open new clubs in locations near to the existing clubs in Chingford and Wanstead. Larkswood Leisure Centre in Chingford became the base for Larkswood Karate Club, and after the classes were well established, I installed Tony Ives, one of our young and very enthusiastic Black Belts as the club instructor there. Waltham Forest 'Pool and Track' became the home of Walthamstow Karate Club. Walthamstow was a success from the very beginning and once again after a few initial teething problems, I installed Salem Tedj as the resident club instructor. Salem had started his karate many years earlier in Algeria. He worked his way through all of the grades at the Wanstead Club and became a Black belt with extremely good technique. A couple of years later when Southbury Leisure Centre was built, the Enfield Club was established, and the late Massoud Aghassi played a big part in helping me start this new club. All of our Black Belts came along for the opening attended by the Mayor of Enfield and Sharon Davies, the Olympic swimmer. We put on a Karate display and gave the public a free Karate lesson. The Enfield club took some time to become established, as so many Karate clubs followed our lead and began their own operations at the same venue shortly after we began. I continued teaching regularly at the Enfield club with my good friend the late Massoud Aghassi, who started out with me as a white belt some twenty years previously. Ironically Southbury Leisure Centre, the home of the Enfield Club, was built on the site of Enfield swimming pool where many years earlier I had had my first fearful and unsuccessful attempts at learning to swim.

Each year, all students and instructors were encouraged to take part in the annual Karate marathon.

A large hall was booked and students obtained sponsorship from friends and colleagues at work or school. The marathon involved everyone completing as many katas as possible during the three hours of the marathon. The money raised went to various charities suggested by the members and over time in excess of £80.000 was raised for many worthwhile causes.

The Chingford club, based at Rushcroft school, was the main club for Black and Brown belts to attend. We often got visitors from other clubs and students from abroad who discovered where we were and came along for karate classes. A club nearby in Tottenham was in the process of closing down and a group of four of the club's members came to us with a view to continue their training. I was always glad that people found our club, and noticed in this group of four that there was a very attractive lady with very long black hair. The group enrolled with us and started their lessons and I could see that the standard of their karate and of this lady, Lucy, was particularly good. The club in Tottenham although now closed down, must have had a very good instructor.

My group of clubs, now called Karate-London, always had an active social life. Parties, meals out and barbecues were regular events, and it was at one of our functions that I socialised with Lucy, who was to become my future wife. The occasion was our 1995 Christmas party held at The Thatched House in Epping. Good food, Greek dancing and entertainment were on offer during the evening. I made a point of going round to the tables to meet all of our members and make sure everyone was having a good time. Towards the end of the evening and after one or two drinks, I found myself on the dance floor with Lucy. We had never really spoken before but we were having fun dancing as the fast disco music continued into a slow ballad. We came closer and started the slow dancing, chatting away together and laughing as if we were old friends. I didn't notice the music had stopped playing, and so there we were, after all of the other dancers had left the floor and were sitting down, still doing the slow dance and chatting away, completely oblivious to the lack of music and the fact that everyone else was looking at us alone on the dance floor. It was embarrassing for both of us. We met up regularly for a drink and a chat after the Christmas party, and I enjoyed the talks, discussions and the easy way that the conversation flowed. There was no agenda for either of us as we were both still married, although separated and living independent lives.

We both however became divorced, and after ten years went by, I proposed to Lucy and we were married on 23rd June 2007 in Waltham Abbey Church. It was a happy occasion with both of our families and friends attending the ceremony and the party afterwards. But as you can see further on, a lot happened between the years 2000 and 2007.

In Waltham Abbey Church on our wedding day, 23rd June 2007

In the West End, legal action began. The lease of the Karate Dojo at Marshall St was to be reclaimed early from Sensei Enoeda by Westminster City Council, and this meant that in the year 2000 the Marshall St Karate Club had to move out of its home, a place that it had inhabited for around 35 years. There were contracts and leases to negotiate legally, and to obtain the dojo premises, the Council had to go to Court in order to settle with the lease holder, Sensei Enoeda. The Marshall St building was old and needed modernising and rebuilding, this was at least the reason the council and its legal team had given for reclaiming the building. There were protests and meetings, action groups and committees, all of which did no good. The council took the building over and it lay derelict and unused for years until finally reopening in 2010 - a full ten years after its initial closure. I attended all of the classes on the very last day of training at the Marshall St dojo and we had a picture taken to record the sad event. Together with other members I helped to move most of the items out of the dojo office and into storage. The reception area displayed framed magazine front covers, old photos of Sensei Enoeda and Nakayama, and the trophies from years of competition, that I had carefully presented and displayed as proud evidence of the club's history, and my almost extinct display skills. These items and memorabilia were carefully dismantled and packed away. The dojo was to be relocated at two venues; The Oasis at Convent Garden and The Budokwai at Kensington. We were all knocked out of orbit by the uprooting of our great Karate club and it must have made Sensei Enoeda immeasurably sad, although he did his best to never show it.

Some of the students continued their training at the Budokwai and some including myself relocated to The Oasis, some left and discontinued their training altogether. Sensei Enoeda did not take classes at either of these venues but tried to start up a completely new West End club in a sports centre called 'The Third Space' - very close to Piccadilly. The centre was brand new, hi tech, with every new gadget and facility available; a boxing ring, a high altitude chamber, studios for various therapies and a combat or martial arts studio. I spent quite a few sad lunchtimes at the venue with Sensei Enoeda, anticipating a small but keen surge of karate students.

The surge never materialised, and due to the high prices of the membership and classes, the venture at The Third Space was eventually discarded. I however, continued training and teaching regularly at The Oasis located near to Holborn.

The Chingford Club based at Rushcroft School moved from its beautiful pine lined dojo into a large sports hall recently built in the playground of the school. The sports hall was like a large aircraft hanger and it was difficult to get any sort of atmosphere in such a big cold building. The move was made in the year 2000 and the new venue proved to be unlucky for Chingford Karate Club. Numbers of club members increased as we utilised the new and larger space, but in 2003 a bombshell dropped.

We were due to host our annual big December course in 2002 with Sensei Enoeda. The posters and tickets were printed and enquiries were coming in from far afield. A couple of weeks before the course I was contacted by Mrs Chieko Buck who was the PA and secretary to Sensei Enoeda. Chieko explained that Sensei Enoeda was returning to Japan for some health treatment and so a replacement instructor would be sent along to take the course. Sensei Otake came over from Greece. We had never seen or heard of him before, but he did a good course which everyone enjoyed. I considered that the problems with Sensei Enoeda's health would be minor; I had after all accompanied him recently to his consultant in Harley St, and after making a subtle enquiry I was told by Sensei Enoeda that, "everything is fine."

On the evening of Friday 29th March 2003 the telephone rang and I was told by a colleague in Australia that Sensei Enoeda had died in Japan. There had been a relapse after an operation and he had gone. It was a total shock. The news quickly spread and the whole of the following day was filled with telephone enquiries asking for details of what had happened and if the news was true. Everyone in the karate world was in shock. How could this have happened to Enoeda - 'The Tiger'- one who was so strong, so full of life, so dynamic and charismatic? The loss of Sensei Enoeda reverberated around the world for a very long time.

A memorial course was organised by the KUGB and held at Crystal Palace Sports Centre, the home of Sensei Enoeda's Spring and Summer courses. Students and instructors from far and wide came and paid their respects by training on the course. One of the saddest jobs I had to do was arrange a memorial table in the Crystal Palace sports hall with pictures of Sensei Enoeda and Sensei Tabata, who had also recently passed away. I used white silk and black ribbon, and together with two framed photographs, I formed a temporary memorial which remained in place until the memorial course training had finished. With candles and incense burning, it was an extremely sobering way to remember these two great instructors who had taught us all in this large sports venue so many times.

Over many years, Sensei Enoeda had hosted dozens of Spring and Summer courses at Crystal Palace. Students from all around the world gathered there each year to train under great names such as Nakayama, Tabata, Tsuyama, Osaka, Kase, Shirai, Yahara, Tanaka and dozens of other top instructors. Visitors from far and wide would arrive and enjoy the Karate and camaraderie of these great twice yearly events, taking in the atmosphere and the unique and individual concepts and applications of Karate. It was now truly the end of an era.

It was not long before the power play started. Who was going to replace Enoeda, the late Chief Instructor of the KUGB and the JKA in Europe? The 'Southern faction' wanted Mr Ohta to claim the JKA crown and the 'Northern faction' wanted Andy Sherry. This geographical split in allegiances was not total, and there were students and instructors from both the North and South who did not necessarily follow these geographical tendencies or loyalties. Karate London followed Mr, Ohta who was Sensei Enoeda's assistant instructor. I was straightway co-opted onto the JKA committee with Ohta and some other long term Enoeda students (although I did have reservations about the speed at which everything was being organised). It was obvious that Mr Ohta had his eye firmly on becoming the replacement Chief Instructor of Great Britain. Dozens of clubs and instructors were against this, and a meeting was called between the leaders of the KUGB and the JKA hierarchy who flew in from Japan for the meeting. The acrimonious, loud and heated meeting was held at the Crystal Palace Sports Centre. Nothing was agreed, but the JKA insisted that their man, Ohta, would be the next Chief Instructor. Andy Sherry and the senior KUGB instructors had been practising Karate with Sensei Enoeda years before Ohta arrived in the UK, and they were naturally not of the opinion that he would be leading something that they had so successfully built up. The JKA decided not to recognise the senior grades that had been awarded by Sensei Enoeda to the highest ranking KUGB instructors. The KUGB subsequently resigned from the JKA which created to two factions in Great Britain - the KUGB and the JKA. The enormous split in the original Karate Union Of Great

Britain could not have been more distinct and divisive and the decision by me to follow Ohta and the JKA had further repercussions later on for the clubs that formed Karate London.

Many people were close to Sensei Enoeda, lots of them more so than I. He had a way of making people feel special, and so we were all close to him in many different ways. The mourning that I experienced during this time was manifest in writing. I put together a book of condolence published on the internet, I had it printed and bound and gave it as a limited edition to Mrs Enoeda and her family. I also completed my tribute book describing the life and times of Sensei Enoeda. Many people, including the highly respected Sensei Tomita, who was an earlier assistant to Sensei Enoeda, helped by contributing pictures and stories to the book. After unsuccessfully trying to find a publisher who would publish the book in full colour, I decided to publish the book myself. 'Keinosuke Enoeda ~ Tiger of Shotokan Karate' was printed in Singapore and finally published in 2005 with a book launch held at The Peter May Sports Centre in Walthamstow. I learnt an awful lot about printing, packaging, design, distribution, percentages, customs and shipping during the time prior to actual publication. Once published, the book became very successful and orders came in from countries all over the world. I made sure that Mrs Enoeda got paid a commission from each book sold; she certainly helped me and gave me her permission for the book to be published. I would not have completed and published the work without her blessing.

I had not realised the effect that following Mr Ohta - the new Chief Instructor of JKA England, would have on my own club members. I considered that there would be opportunities for everyone in the newly formed breakaway group now called JKA England. I was wrong! Most of our experienced students and instructors were involved with the KUGB, regularly traveling up to Liverpool to train with the KUGB junior and adult squads. Having relinquished our membership of the KUGB meant that this opportunity was now lost. There was a mutiny, and a number of my students and instructors decided not to follow in the direction that our clubs were taking. They wanted to continue with the squad training with a view to winning the KUGB National Championships. I felt that my loyalty, although in retrospect misguided, was to follow Mr Ohta and continue with my teaching and my studies at The Oasis in London. I considered that there would be opportunities for us all in the new group whereas there were few opportunities for us all in the KUGB. Resignations followed; Tony, David, Steven, Mike and Barbara Ives, Donna Kilroy, Tim Ahmet, Jason and Samantha Plumb and Billy Merrifield, all left to continue in the KUGB with many of their friends and training colleagues subsequently following them. These members were in the Chingford Club team, and some were club instructors who often helped in the classes. They were all important in different ways, and after nurturing these students for twenty years or so from white belt up to Black Belt and beyond, and assisting them with their own development as Karate instructors and competitors, I certainly questioned the meaning of loyalty and how loyalty is served.

Following Mr Ohta and JKA England proved to be an upsetting and divisive decision but it was a decision that I had to make. I never really considered that the KUGB had anything to offer the older student or dedicated instructor. A very limited number of National and International Champions did well in the KUGB, becoming grading examiners and forming part of an elite group of Nationally respected instructors. This luxury was not available to the average student or instructor who had not gained National or International status on the competition circuit. I was certainly confused and concerned at this time; the death of Sensei Enoeda, the split in the organisation of Karate, and the ensuing problems that occurred in the JKA, all gave me plenty of sleepless nights.

It was 2004, and I noticed that within the JKA England committee there were often petty arguments, reprimands and rather silly rumours whispered about one thing or another, or gossip spread about some innocent instructor or student. Letters and even legal threats were sent out ad hoc to instructors and students who were considered to be 'rocking the boat' in some way, or causing some imaginary problem. I was subjected to petty jealousy and victimisation, probably due to the success of the clubs I was running and lots of interest in the forthcoming Enoeda book.

The Gods certainly had conspired to present me with success from many different quarters, but the JKAE didn't like it. I was riding on the crest of a wave at the time, travelling to Eton each week teaching Karate to the sons of Royalty and the rich and famous at Eton College. One of my students - Tim Ahmet, had already become the National under 21 Kumite Champion whilst we were in the KUGB and now I had another; Daniel Jenkinson won this title and was chosen to represent JKA England in the World Shotokan Karate Championships to be held in Japan. I was also chosen to run with the Olympic Torch Relay in England as the torch continued its journey to the Olympic Games to be held in Athens. My part of the Olympic Torch Relay started at 'Lords' cricket ground where the roads were crowded both sides with people cheering and waving Union Jack flags. It was a wonderful experience that was later on slightly spoilt by the silliness of the new JKA that I had become part of. Letters of warning, faxes and reprimands were regularly sent out to long standing Enoeda students who had joined the new group, some of whom had been training for thirty years or more under Sensei Enoeda. Mr Ohta, the new Chief Instructor, became disliked as he was seen as the person responsible for much of this unwarranted and unnecessary hostile action (much of which I believe was and is due, to his own paranoia and insecurity). He was surrounded by sycophants who refused to criticise him or suggest that his way of doing things was generally not supported. I spoke to him personally and explained that he would lose members if he continued in this way. Nothing changed. This was not really my idea of how a Karate organisation should be administered, and it was not long before I myself started to receive words of warning for some completely innocent action, or questioned about rumours that had been spread maliciously around. Eventually my own students started to receive the same kind of treatment with warning letters and even telephone calls to them at work. It was a nightmare. I was caught in a trap of my own making and decided to explain and discuss the situation to my senior Black Belts.

The choices were stark. We could go on as we were and hope that things would improve, or we could return to the KUGB or even a different established Karate organisation. There was a third choice though, but this was not one that I really wanted to take; we could form our own Karate organisation. Karate clubs do not change organisations or affiliations on a whim. Licences, documents, courses, gradings and most of the other administration has to be renewed or changed completely. The decision at that time to form our own group was not taken by me but by our Black Belts, and I endorsed their decision. We subsequently resigned from JKA England. I resigned from the Oasis karate club and also resigned from my position as chairman of the Oasis Club committee. I lost some good friends in the Oasis Karate Club and the committee, but before resigning I recommended Florence Hands - one of the senior Oasis students - for the position of Chairman of the committee. She remained in that position for a good number of years before moving abroad.

As a group of successful Karate Clubs, we were now in uncharted territory, but I knew that with the support and backing of my Black Belts, I could make the necessary push forward to make all of our ideas come to fruition, and there were ideas - loads of them. We had seen the mistakes and weaknesses of the big organisations, and now we had our own chance to do things fairly, honestly and properly. The idea of *Shotokan Karate England* was formed at a meeting held at Wanstead Leisure Centre on Monday 24th January 2005 with all of our Black Belts in attendance. The plan to strike out alone was unanimous.

The first inaugural committee meeting of SKE was held on Sunday 6th February 2005. During the subsequent years, we have all had opportunities to challenge ourselves with the events that we have organised. None of us would have had these opportunities in the KUGB or the JKA, and so I feel confident that we have made the correct decisions when we had to. We have now been joined by other like-minded clubs and instructors, some of whom were original Marshall St members, and so consequently SKE has grown considerably. Years after becoming the Great Britain under 21 Kumite champion, Tim Ahmet has also now returned and helps teaching at the clubs based in East London. I organised a small course for him to host and it was an overwhelming success. I am very proud of him as a person, a student and a teacher. I am in the honourable position of being the Chief Instructor of Shotokan Karate England, and together with the effort and work that I have to put into this position, feel humbled by the dedication of the many students and instructors regularly training and teaching. In spite of this growth, I still like to consider that we are 'small' and can act effectively like a team or a small organization, rather than a big monolithic Karate association. Everyone is important in SKE, and I like to include all of the senior Black Belts in the running of the organisation, it doesn't matter if they are competition champions or not. Everyone has something unique to offer, give or teach.

As well as the disappointments, Karate certainly has given me an awful lot of pleasure; the times with Sensei Enoeda and the wonderful people I have met from all around the world; the new and the old friends whose company I greatly enjoy; the loyalty, gratitude and respect that has been given to me; my wife Lucy and the great times together that we have shared, are all the result of a very successful Karate life. My relationship with Lucy grew during these years and we were happily married on 23rd June 2007.

There has been pain too; the first student I 'grew' from beginner to Black Belt - a gifted child of just eight years, who learnt quicker than any adult - made Black Belt in just three years, an almost unheard of accomplishment. A week after his successful Black Belt grading, he arrived early in the class to casually tell me he was finishing karate. I considered that he must be going away on holiday, but he explained that he was finishing now that he had got his Black Belt! There have been many others too, some silently leaving without even a whisper or a goodbye after you have guided them for many years. Then there was the young lad, a quiet diligent student who trained hard, worked and sweated week after week in the dojo and struggled privately with his own personal demons, before finally throwing himself under a train to end his life. You have to be strong as an instructor and you have to deal with many problems and challenges as and when they come along.

I don't understand everything that has happened or why, but it has been an incredible journey. Karate has certainly been an educator to me, and in spite of the pain and frustration often felt, there is a wonderful sense of achievement and I would recommend Karate training to everyone.

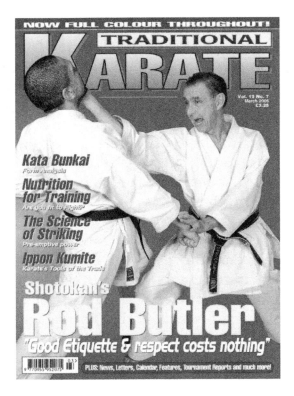

FAMILY

'Luck is the result of endeavour' - unknown

M y Mother lives on in most things I do and say. The pearls of wisdom imparted by her years ago, as if they were universal truths, to my Sister and myself, and mostly gleaned from the daily newspapers, stick in my mind like milestones or signposts on a long pedestrian journey. 'Today's Thought' - a small paragraph of wisdom published daily, was snipped carefully from the newspaper and religiously pinned to a display board in the kitchen for all to see and take heed of, usually accompanied by a finger waved as a warning sign. There were dozens of these newspaper snippets on the board, and the very old ones had to be taken down to make way for the new daily intake. Old ones were relegated to a box on the mantlepiece for further possible use in the future. We took this 'Today's Thought' habit for granted as we sighed and our eyes looked skywards, but of course what our Mother was trying to do was guide us in the right direction with our lives. She didn't have the support of a loving husband and we didn't have a real father, but she did her best and cared for us both, in her own special way. I like to think she was successful, and often say a prayer of thanks to her for her guidance. She encouraged good table manners, and a lifetime later it still irks me to see bad table manner. 'Manners maketh the man' is not such a bad proverb, but unfortunately good manners are practised more in the USA than over here in England nowadays.

Years later I still find myself distributing anecdotes to youngsters in a karate class or to anyone else who I consider may benefit from a few words prised from my subconscious; 'It's the early bird that (catches the worm)' - I actually wait for the students in the class to finish the line, although the phrase 'Don't spoil the ship (for a hap'orth of tar)' does result in blank faces and quizzical expressions. 'There's many a slip 'twixt cup and lip,' usually prompts a few odd looks and enquiries. I subconsciously listen out for any new phrases that I have not heard before and even create my own, such is the habit. 'It'll all end in tears' is one that my Mother usually dispensed habitually if and when I disclosed a new and unapproved of hobby, relationship or activity. 'The silent sow sucketh the most swill,' is one that I use for special effect when someone is treating me to a dose of verbal diarrhoea. 'It'll be alright in the end, and if it's not alright, it's not the end' is my favourite at the moment. If my Mother saw me making an effort in any activity or direction, she would always encourage me with the words 'More power to your elbow' – I can't imagine the origins of that one!

Of course my subsequent family life has never materialised as I expected it to. Lucy and I have a good marriage; a good life, we don't really need for anything. Lucy's son and daughter Daniel and Lisa, call round quite regularly, and I try to make them feel as comfortable as possible. I feel as though I should make an extra effort for them as they don't have a father around - at least not one in this country who they can go to visit. I get on with them both well, and in actual fact I have a kind of respect for their own efforts in life and the way that they have accepted me.

The break up of any marriage has far reaching effects on the family members involved, and this must be true of all family break ups. Damage is there, and it is difficult to mend. Lucy has made a big effort to keep the remaining family links with her son and daughter in good working order. My own divorce certainly increased the stresses and tensions that were there previously, and it has been difficult to resolve these issues with my own son and daughter. I wonder what Rod Stewart's secret is; he has moved from one marriage to another with children along the way, over a period of three or four decades, and all of his many fragmented family members seem to get along famously. I imagine that 'celebrity' must have something to do with it - people act differently in the presence of a celebrity, they may 'go the extra mile' or make the extra effort that may be expected, requested or required.

There is however, (in 2012), a wind of change rustling through the branches of my own family life. Things are thankfully much better now. Both Simone, and Daren with his family, now visit Lucy and I at home. Trips out or meals at home are arranged and thankfully the stress of previous years has dissipated. The two grandchildren, Wolfie and Drake enjoy these visits and family times too, and it makes me very happy to see them laughing and playing together.

The road back was difficult. For many years there was a big gap in my heart. Although I had great relationship with Lucy, my children were not there, not in my life, not in our life. I hoped there would be a phone call, a card or a letter, but for around fifteen years there was anger and emptiness. I tried at various times to engineer meetings to sort out perceived problems and grudges, but the meetings always seemed uncomfortable, sitting in a pub or in a car, and none of these meetings that were supposed to mend things, worked; it was not the right time. Isn't it strange just how important timing is in your life?

Dwelling on this makes me feel sorry for myself and gives me a feeling of deja-vu - well, it did happen earlier on in my life with my first wife and my Mother. They never got on together and I wonder if it is my fault that my own family members didn't mix together and form something greater than its individual constituents. I tell myself reluctantly that some things cannot be changed, some things have to be accepted.

However, as I said, things are changing for the better. For one week in 2012 Simone and Lisa travelled with Lucy, Jan, Rachel (Lucy's Sister) and myself for a one week holiday in Kefalonia, Greece. After the initial tensions dismissed themselves, it was a great week and lots of fun was had by all. Simone confided that she enjoyed this short chunk of 'family time' together, and upon returning to England, she landed a job playing bass guitar with 'Primal Scream' an extremely popular and successful rock band. She wanted to play professionally, and now she has a great opportunity. Lucy's daughter Lisa, is also now working and training to become a branch manager at the Nationwide Building Society.

God, wishing to further demonstrate and establish his benevolence, provided me with one more giant chunk of happiness which established the family roots on a much sounder footing. On 9th October 2012 Daren, Elizabeth and their two boys, Wolfie and Drake came around to see Lucy and I at home. It was the first time that we had all properly met together and it was a joyful afternoon with Wolfie inspecting my childhood collection of birds eggs, seashells and other collectables, and Drake laughing and gurgling away happily at all of the proceedings. Since then we have all shared Boxing Day together, opening presents and having fun.

Darren works as a technician with 'The Cure' and has travelled to many countries as the band completes its schedule of shows and festivals. He has also produced and published a book - a Cure discography and has helped to produce films about The Cure on tour. I never encouraged Daren or Simone to go into the music business, but from a very early age, both enjoyed music, especially some of the concerts that I took them to. I took Daren to see 'Madness,' 'Journey' and Toyah Wilcox, Simone went to see 'Take That' and Michael Jackson. These early musical experiences, plus the guitar flavoured environment at home, must have made a mark that has influenced their own ambitions and careers. I never realised there was a musical osmosis filtering through to Daren and Simone, but it is nice that the musical tradition has continued. Simone recently confessed to putting my guitar around her neck and miming when she was a child and when I was not at home, so the clues were there almost as if there were two parallel lives, one of which I knew nothing about.

I have always enjoyed visits to my Sister's home down in Devon where the politics of family life are put away for the duration of the visit. During my first marriage, the visits to Jan's were always enjoyable but there always was a tension coming from my wife, Rita, who didn't really want to be there. Daren, particularly, considered that I was trying to 'show off' whilst on these visits, but in truth I was just enjoying the time away from the stresses and pressures of work, in a different environment and with a family who accepted all of my silliness and my rather tame jokes. Luckily now, the visits to Devon are very enjoyable for Lucy and myself; free of tension, family politics, and fun to boot! We both enjoy these times that are all too rare, the silliness continues but we all just laugh. Jan's large and now extended family enjoy these visits almost as much as we do and there is a wonderful feeling of liberation just being down there. These times are to me, the family times that I have always yearned for so much, and I dream when quietly alone, of how nice it would be for all of the family members to be together and enjoy times like these.

When I sometimes see film of families in France or Italy eating outside, seated along large benches with wine, bread, cheese, ham and so on, I envy them. The sun shines down through a canopy of vine leaves and branches, dappling the children's faces as they all laugh and talk together. The older family members remembering stories and joking, batting rapport back and forth from excited mouths to eager ears, and the younger members giggling and enjoying the food. I envy the freedom that they have to just enjoy the food and their time spent in each other's company. Of course it is an idealistic dream but like the song says, 'If you don't have a dream, how are you going to have a dream come true?' The nearest that I have ever got to having the family all together were on two occasions. My second wedding and my 65th Birthday. The wedding; everyone came, and we all had a beautiful day and evening together. It rained but we all danced, ate and laughed. I didn't get a 60th birthday celebration and so I insisted that we have a big party for my 65th. It was a grand affair which Lucy planned and organised in great detail. She got loads of my friends from years ago to make a surprise entrance at the party. Bimbo from school (together with one of our old textbooks given to me as a present), Richard Stockley came all the way from South Africa for the party, Anne Lantree from the Honeycombs, Peter Pye from the Skylarks, Billy from 'X', and Harry from Zarabanda were just a few of the many faces that have been part of my life over the years. I sang and played a few songs with my guitar and of course the musical highlight for me was Simone playing the bass guitar with me. She was good, and joined in with Billy Ritchie on the keyboards. In just a couple of years she would be touring the World playing bass with 'Primal Scream.'

Gary James, one of our Black Belt instructors, has a great voice and he sung a few songs too. Daren came with his partner, Elizabeth, and their first baby, Wolfie. I made sure that everyone had a room for the night so we could all continue with the revelry at breakfast in the morning. Lucy organised the whole event meticulously; I was truly happy and I think that many others were too.

My 65th Birthday Party with a jam session - Billie Ritchie on keyboards,
my daughter Simone on bass and myself on the left

Above ; my guitar shaped birthday cake. Here I am with Bimbo, Richard Stockley and Lucy above.

My Sister Jan comes up to London once or twice a year. I collect her from Paddington Station, as I used to collect my own Mother years ago when she came up for her annual visit. Jan is then comfortably settled into the spare room with us and we have wonderful times together. Lucy enjoys these times as much as I do and there are always some events planned or arranged; an evening out, a show, a meal and even 'afternoon tea' at the Ritz on one occasion! Sometimes we have a week away together; Lucy and I, Jan and Lucy's Sister Rachel. We have been to Italy, France, Greece and Turkey for these exciting one week excursions. We all get along well and I feel closer to Jan now than ever. She has had a difficult life and it may be that recognising this suffering and her struggle brings us closer. Jan has a fantastic family of grown up children who all visit her regularly and gravitate to her home at special times like birthdays and Christmas. She is very important to me and I feel blessed to have such a Sister and such a very interesting and enjoyable life, not at all bad for a Baby Boomer or War Baby!

In many ways this book has been overtaken by history, as it has taken me so long to finish! During the last ten years, the family has grown with children and grand children. There have been losses too with dear friends and relatives who have passed away. At 76 years of age my work schedule has also changed considerably as I have passed responsibility for most of the Karate Clubs onto other loyal and responsible instructors. This book is, however, a snapshot of my memories written between the years of 2010 and 2020.

It's a good job that I don't make a living from writing; one book every ten years would not provide an income of any sort to pay the bills!

SWIMMING

'All out and up the deep end' - My swimming teacher

T his section has been added towards the end
of the book as swimming is an ongoing pro-
ject, continually changing and challenging, a bit like life
itself. It's good to have fear, and it is great to overcome it.
I always feared water, and from the time of being a baby, I
hated the ordeal of my face being washed, or getting wet
in any way. I didn't like the flannel or the soap anywhere
near me, and this fear or hatred of water has continued
throughout my life, in the past stopping me from learning to swim and enjoy the fun that could be had on the
beach, in the sea or in the swimming pool. I don't know
how this fear developed, but I do manage to wash now,
and sometimes even have a bath; such is my determin-
ation!

It was not until I was fifty years of age that I
finally decided to put paid to this rotten fear and finally
face my lifelong phobia of water. I had already managed to put my head under the water, hold my breath
and swim (I use the word loosely) for a couple of yards
(underneath the water) in a swimming pool. I had no idea
about the technique of the strokes, breathing or for that
matter swimming near the surface of the water. My attempts at swimming would actually be called drowning

by most people who could not understand the suicidal stage of progress that I had reached. (I would however answer; It has taken me 50 years to get this far!) I subsequently started swimming lessons at Arnos Grove Pool, a pool which often seemed quite dirty and occasionally blessed with small brown objects floating around, kindly left by the disabled group who used the pool during the preceding hour. The long handled net did its job well but the class was, more often than not, ushered out of the pool on health and safety grounds after certain objects were found floating in the water or lying on the floor of the pool. I was also not greatly encouraged by one of the swimming teachers who, after I explained the difficulty I had in water, informed me that;

"Some of us are floaters and some of us are sinkers - you're a sinker."

Clever sod, I thought, so I said, sarcastically returning his sneer,

"Well, I must be able to swim to the bottom then!"

Of course his comment was a red flag to me and I decided to try further classes and persevere at other pools. I went to Albany Pool, but the lessons there were given in a children's paddling pool - very embarrassing. I ended up going to the deepest and most fearful pool of all - Southgate! Earplugs, nose-clip and goggles were essential aids that had to accompany me quivering to the water's edge. On arrival, the voice of the large lady swimming instructor teaching the earlier class put the fear of God into me, even though I was only in the changing room and not even in my trunks yet. I used to arrive thirty minutes before the class, just to build courage enough to get into the water. She was a fearful lady. By the time I got near the water, I was a quivering wreck. I thought long and hard about what it must feel like to drown with her voice shouting through the water at you - the last words you would ever hear before drowning. I never did but I nearly did, many times.

However, she did get me through with her bullying, to swim; sculling and backstroke first, then gliding to the side, then kicking with a float, then treading water and then, nightmare of nightmares; "All out and up to the deep end!" The words I dreaded. We all had to climb out of the relatively safe shallow end with just four feet of water, walk to the far end of the pool and jump in at the deep end! A bottomless ocean and a completely alien terrain into which we were all being encouraged, as if we were lemmings, to commit suicide. I considered that the best form of equipment for this depth of water would be a submarine. I was always the last person in the group to jump or should I say fall into the water. As I waited, last in the line of ten rather well built ladies, the panic rose. I instructed the swimming teacher to bring the long pole with a hook at one end, near to the edge. All of the other learners had by now swum to the far end and were happily laughing at me as I fell in and quickly grabbed the pole with both hands. I wasn't going to wimp out and so went through this water torture every week, until one particular week when there was a children's swimming competition that took over our side of the pool. We had to have our class on the opposite side of the pool, and when the command "all out and up to the deep end" came, I knew that I would be unable to fall in and grab the pole that was usually on my right hand side; there would be no 'right hand side.' The ladies jumped, dived and belly flopped, all making it to the far end. This was it;

I jumped in, surfaced, turned quickly onto my back and did the back stroke to the far end of the pool amid cheers from the rest of the class. I did it. For the first time ever, I swam a length of the Southgate pool. My confidence slowly grew week by week in each of those Sunday lessons. I picked up the breast stroke quite easily and then the crawl, which I still find difficult, but at least now, if I ever drown, I will drown more slowly and enjoyably, and appreciate more fully the water rushing past me as I breast stroke or attempt to crawl, to the bottom of the deep end.

The irony of all of this is quite amazing; On returning to Arnos Grove Pool for a few extra classes, the improvement in my swimming was noticed. I was encouraged to enter the annual swimming competition and somehow agreed to take part in the event which was to take place at, you've guessed it - Southgate Pool. My only two possible strokes for the competition were Breast Stroke and Back Stroke (I hadn't got the crawl properly at all), but this didn't seem to dampen the enthusiasm of the Arnos Grove swimming team and the team coach. I was put into the Breast Stroke, Back Stroke and freestyle events and then the Team Relay Event! Quite ridiculous I thought.

All of the other contestants were good strong swimmers - with special trunks and googles, legs shaved hairless for speed and not wearing surfing shorts printed with seagulls, like me. The big day arrived, and for all of the events, I kind of shuffled into the water and did my best to get to the other end. I remember being beaten in one of these events by a man with one leg doing the crawl, whilst I did the Breast stroke, such was my speed and skill in the water! I was last in the team relay and of course reached the finish point minutes after all of the other teams, but I was being cheered and clapped by an extremely enthusiastic Arnos Grove team. I couldn't understand all of the fuss, as I was last in all of the events, but later on I discovered that taking part in all of the events of the day had provided the team with valuable points - points which, if they didn't have, would have placed them in a much lower position in the swimming club rankings. The competition was a team success!

* * *

As well as my fear of water discovered at an early age, there was also another daily ordeal during early childhood that I had to endure, and that was; going to the toilet. The toilet was outside in the garden and so it was always a cold, damp and not very inviting place. Inside, hanging on the wall, was the toilet paper. 'Bronco' was the proud name stamped across the wrapping, together with a picture of a wild bull (or was it a horse?) in a charging position! One can only speculate as to how the manufacturers considered a wild bull or horse and the name 'Bronco' would begin to describe a toilet paper made for use in the most intimate and personal of places. Bronco came in single sheets or a roll. If you were lucky, there would be a roll hanging up. If not, you would have to try to negotiate with single sheets, which in any case were like very rough sand paper, and seemed like a punishment to you for ever having considered going to the toilet. Bronco toilet paper must have been a residual product left over from the war years. I imagine that these single sheets were used sparingly by the army in the war, with the Sergeant Major shouting at the reluctant soldier in the latrines using his daily ration;

"Three sheets only - one for up, one for down and one to shine!"

I hated going to the toilet and found that I could put off the dreadful event with the result that later on I would end up with terrible stomach pains and the doctor would have to be called.

A few years later we built a 'lean to' onto the rear of the house at 7 Millais Rd which meant that we didn't have to go outside in the wind and the rain to visit the toilet. Regardless of this luxury, we still retained the services of good old Bronco.

'Lifebuoy' was the name of the soap that was in general use. I suppose that in this case, manufacturers must have considered that B.O. was so dangerous that 'Lifebuoy' toilet soap would miraculously come to the rescue in order to save your life. A lot of these old names and words have now disappeared. I remember my real Father buying '7 O'Clock' razors from Woolworths. I remember the 'Copper' where clothes were boiled clean, and the 'Wringer' where clothes were wrung dry after being washed. 'Mantles' had to be fixed around the gas lights in the ceiling and they tended to flare up if they needed replacing. There was of course the 'Range', which would heat the home and cook the meals at the same time, and the trusty 'pig bin' doing its weekly favour to man and animal alike with its recycling of all old food matter; everything from potato peelings to apple cores went into the pig bin.

'Spills', made out of tightly twisted newspaper would start the fire in place of wood which was expensive, and the 'Toasting Fork' would be used to make toast out of a slice of bread held close to the open fire, later to be covered with a lovely thick layer of jam. Robertsons Jam had a Gollywog on the jam jar label as their trademark. Labels from the jam jar could be saved and then sent off to the manufacturer, and in exchange for these labels, the sender would receive in the post a beautiful enamel and brass Gollywog badge. These Gollywog badges were a kind of status symbol, proudly worn by many of the children at school. A victim of our racial political correctness, these Gollywog badges have disappeared, and those remaining are probably now collectors items. Gollywogs were held with the same affection as Teddy Bears or dolls by all young children, oblivious to the revulsion and angst that has now been encouraged and propagated by our governments for their own perverted reasons.

'Cornflakes,' 'Marmite,' 'Spam' and 'Corned Beef' seem to have survived and bridged the generation gap, but 45s, 78s, LPs, EPs, Fablon and Auto-changers have not been so lucky. I imagine MP3s, Blogs and Email will go the same way, and their disappearance will also be mourned by the youth of today in later years. I am sure that each generation has its own sentimental memories of things that made them happy or possibly fearful during childhood and the growing up years. Whatever happened to Tizer or the bottles of Corona delivered by truck to every home requiring their weekly supply of pop or, whatever became of 'The Bogey Man?'

At this point the text segues into Part Two because as I am sure you have noted, I have started to rant.......

PART TWO

RANT

**'It's not what you've got, it's what
you *do* with what you've got' - Rod Butler**

I t would be quite easy for me to leave this section out, to press the delete button for this chapter, as I would not want to upset or alienate anyone, any friend or relative; but that is the whole point. Why are we so upset by other peoples' points of view? We used to be able to say what we felt about anything, or anyone. I am not a hateful person and it is not my intention to encourage others to hate, but, surely I am allowed to say what I feel without others running for their politically correct dictionary? It used to be the case where people of differing opinions listened, talked and accepted or discussed the opinion of others. Disagreements or arguments would take place and each protagonist would possibly be enlightened, or at the least, entertained. My mind goes back to the time when I was working in the nursery. It was a 'closed shop' – meaning everyone had to be in the Union - (NUPE). There would be many enjoyable political discussions as most of the nursery workers were staunch Left Wing advocates, and one was even a Shop Steward, but a few of us leaning towards the Right would engage. Enjoyable, entertaining and enlightening banter would ensue. Not so today. If a person has a differing opinion it is like a declaration of war with little chance of a friendly exchange of opinions. If you cannot bear to hear an opinion that maybe different to your own, then please do not read this chapter.

From early childhood, although afflicted with severe shyness, I was always opinionated. I remember explaining to an older boy who told me there was no such thing as God, the reasons that *I* considered there *was* God. I must have been around seven years old and he must have discovered that I went to Church. "Look at the trees and birds" I explained, "there must be a God or how would these things get here?" On another occasion, a lad was telling me that his family was waiting for a new Council House. I found this strange and innocently asked him "Why are you waiting for the council to give you a house, why don't you get one yourself?" I can't remember his response and I don't really know where my innocent cheek came from, but I still have that cheek and still manage to occasionally say the wrong thing at the wrong time. I just assumed from a very early age that we are all in control of our own destiny; if we want something we have to reach out and work slowly towards it. I am at this point in history, a minority, as anyone who speaks so directly and in such an un-vetoed manner is not considered normal. 'Unfiltered' is the word used to describe this kind of direct talk today.

I think that the English have now entered a period of sterile conformity and fear. We have to adhere to 'political correctness' whereby we cannot joke, think or talk about anything that might offend the delicately porcelain sensitivities of the public in general or our political leaders. Jokes about an 'Englishman an Irishman and a Scotsman' are now frowned upon as if a blasphemous and unforgivable sin had been committed. Jokes from comedians about the eccentricities of various races are now dusty and redundant, together with some of the old TV sit-coms which mocked various races and religions. Jokes about Jews or Arabs are banned from our thoughts and words, as are jokes or conversations about God, Homosexuals or prostitutes. We cannot say 'mankind', 'manmade' or 'chairman' for that would offend female sensitivities. Words like 'Humankind,' 'Person-made' or 'Chair-Person' are much less insulting or upsetting. It may be that words like 'whitewash' will also eventually find their way into the politically incorrect dictionary. I find it amazing that government duties, instead of maintaining the defence of our country, maintaining good education, law and order, and keeping our country clean and tidy, now include the daily minutia of what we are allowed to think and say.

Part of the problem is our overuse of the adjective. A blithe description such as xenophobe, sexist, racist or misogonist, dismisses a colleague or friend with such ferocity that most are unwilling or cant be bothered to return the compliment or take the conversation any further. However, the racism that we see worldwide in football today is genuine and unacceptable to most of the civilised world. This racism is particularly nasty as it is used to undermine the skills of a player or a team and upset the success of that player or team. I am sure it often has the opposite effect.

We are not supposed to laugh at a man with a bowler hat and umbrella, a man with a kilt and sporran, or an Arab wearing desert attire to keep the sand and heat at bay, on a cold winter's day in London's Oxford St. In fact we shouldn't laugh at any person wearing strange or comical clothes, as this will offend their 'human rights' or their personal 'dignity'. I still laugh though. We now, with government guidance, carefully veto everything we think, and certainly everything we say in public. Certain jokes received by email are passed on to some but not to others who may be 'sensitive.' Speeches in the media by political parties that offend the public consensus or indoctrinated view of what is correct and acceptable, are excluded from general discussion and opinion. I find this control over our thoughts and words unhealthy and disturbing. There is an actual fear that something said in a lighthearted or jovial manner may result in a visit from the Police, instigated by some upstanding member of the politically correct public. In fact as I write this, the law in Scotland has been changed in order to prevent people saying certain things in the privacy of their own home! On the other side of the coin there is also a (possibly paranoid) fear that something said *may* touch a nerve of public awareness or strike a chord and awaken the country to the realisation of what is actually taking place; mind and even thought control.

The government wishes to stamp out any spark of dissent before it starts an avalanche of disapproval. Have we lost our perhaps old fashioned British humour, the humour where we laugh at each other regardless of race, sexual tendancy or religion? I think the answer must be 'Yes.'

Commentators and the public are reluctant to actually bring into the open considerations and concerns that much of the public actually (secretly) has. The result of this is the example of the tragedy of Norway in 2011 when Anders Breivick murdered 77 people in order to make his point heard, against a backdrop of public shock and horror that he should even *think* such things. If the public and the politicians *had* talked about such things, this would never have happened. The lid was kept on and the pot boiled over. I don't think he was purely insane, I think he was determined to put his point over in a way that the authorities had to listen to. He believed that there was a conspiracy in the political hierarchy that enabled many Islamic visitors to settle in the country and exert their own rules and culture within Norway and Europe, without any consideration for the ethnic population. He may have had a point. It is not so far-fetched when one looks at the corruption of political leaders in many countries that overrule their domestic responsibilities. I am sure there is corruption in our own country, as I see the unbalanced influx of immigrants into England, when there are not enough school places, roads, shops, doctors' surgeries, hospitals or houses to accommodate them all. Just why have our political leaders quietly arranged this? Why have they not explained their reasoning? The normal knee jerk reaction of the public is that a comment or a question such as this is racist and there is a swift intake of breath through lips, which are shaped as if starting a word beginning with a 'W'. As such, there should be no further discussion on the matter; it is pushed under the carpet, ignored or diverted into a more acceptable and 'soft' subject of discussion, with the perpetrator of the comment simply labeled a 'racist,' or the more modern pronunciation of the word; 'rayshist.' My God! Are we living in Aldous Huxley's Brave New World?

I am not advocating, murder, terrorism or rioting to get a point across, and naturally I do not condone violence in any form to propagate one's point of view. I am not suggesting that Breivick be applauded for his terrible act of mass murder. I *am* suggesting that we open up and give ourselves permission to *talk* about things that everyone seems to shy away from. Let us talk, listen, laugh and decide what we think is correct before there is another big explosion, another car bomb or another mass murder. Any politician who dares to do this will be ostracised by his party but will be applauded by much of the general public. We all have opinions and that is what they are, opinions, they are not necessarily the truth or fact, but I believe we need to listen to each other's opinions and not just label each other with a tag shutting down one of life's greatest enjoyments; conversation.

The media seem to be on the side of the terrorists. The day after an off duty soldier was murdered - hacked to death by a ranting religious fanatic, BBC television gave airtime to a Muslim preacher of hate, who refused to denounce the murderer and his actions.

I believe that there is a thin and fragile conformity that holds our civilisation together. Politicians like to make us all think everything is fine; everything is OK. But they are scared. Scared that the fragile bond that binds us will break and there will be anarchy. It has almost happened a couple of times and the Police have had to use heavy-handed tactics to control groups of rioting anarchists.

The one thing that scares our leaders, particularly those in America, is Rock n Roll. Jim Morrison, The Doors, John Lennon and The Rolling Stones, together with others, were all candidates considered by governments to be dangerous and able to incite unrest in the cosy environment that had been created. They were hunted down by the Police, keen to earn badges of honour by detaining and interrupting the perceived corruption of civilisation by these musicians. Rock n Roll did cause a revolution in the 50s. Flower Power did the same in the 60s. Disco had little political effect, but Punk in the 80s did worry a lot of our leaders. We have to conform. Music can change things and the politicians know that. They worry.

Political differences however do run very deep. In the UK we each have our political preferences, but in the USA these preferences are much more pronounced and run much deeper. I witnessed this first hand when I was on a one week Karate course in Philladelphia. The sleeping quarters was a large dormitory filled with some of the most senior karate instructors in the USA. The arguing between the Democrats and the Republicans went on all night long with very heated arguments nearly every night. During the day the arguments were forgotten and everyone continued with their Karate training as normal.

One of the saddest things I heard was an interview with the one remaining Everly Brother, Don Everly. The Everly Brothers music was, and still is, loved by everyone, although the duo had not spoken for many years. Don explained that they would always struggle to get on together as one was a Democrat and the other a Republican. A very sad situation which contributed towards their years of working apart and not talking to each other.

*   *   *

There are prosecutions every month against internet users and the language that they use on the 'social media' websites such as Twitter or Facebook. There must be a herd of government officials who watch these websites 24 hours a day, waiting for some unsuspecting author to publish a word or a phrase that they consider to be unacceptable. I think it is ridiculous that we have to be so careful and the authorities so very sensitive to words that are just that – words – an opinion on a computer screen. Fight back. If someone calls you a dummy then call them a 'double dummy'.

There have been riots in our own country because certain subjects are not up for discussion. Politicians have their own agenda, and will reach the conclusion that suits them, not the one that actually addresses the problem. Difficult or unpopular solutions are avoided, as it is important for the politician or council to stay in power and be seen to retain their 'political correctness,' thus, instead of building more hospitals, schools and doctors' surgeries, they build more houses! The same goes for the legal system where terrorists and criminals are treated as welcome guests in the country, whilst judges, lawyers and solicitors obtain obscene incomes as they argue against all common sense that the terrorist or criminal's 'human rights' are being abused because they are threatened with conviction, jail or deportation for their crimes.

The media - TV and film, have been given 'guidelines' on how they should perform, appear and relate to the public. The result being that we are forced to watch infantile adverts about serious matters such as insurance, health and investments. All TV advertising and programming now has to include various ethnicities in the cast of the show or advert to make us all feel 'comfortable' about the 'multicultural' society that now surrounds us. We are meant to feel 'this is how it is, isn't it wonderful?' Years ago we all got on well with each other and didnt need prodding by the media to encourage us how to think or act. I wonder how long it will be before two eyes are staring at us through a black hooded veil as the 'News at Ten' is read to us. Many of us see through this pseudo world created for us by the government and media.

I find it sad that after decades working in Karate and in music, mixing with every race and every religion, we now have to 'label' each other and consider ethnicity. People are chosen for jobs or opportunity based on their sex, their social background or the colour of their skin. We never used to think of black or white, we just loved the music of Chuck Berry or Fats Domino, we loved the sport of Muhammad Ali or the news broadcasts of Trevor McDonald. Indeed rock music broke down much of the racism that there was in the USA with musicians refusing to play to segregated audiences. In Karate and in music, one is respected for their ability, their attitude, their honesty or their kindness. We have never ever considered colour; black or white, gay or lesbian. People were friends or work colleagues and were blind to race, colour or sexual tendency. Now that the government and the media have force fed us for so long the notion that racism is bad, we are more racist than ever before. People don't like being preached to by those above us with money and power, who dont live in the real world that we inhabit.

It is not unusual to see the Police being investigated for a comment that one of them has made and it is certainly not uncommon for the Police to investigate a comment that a member of the public has made or added to one of the 'social media' websites. The Police are certainly not perfect and, as you have read, I had early experience of this imperfection in my teenage years. We are all 'offended' by anything that anyone can say about just about everything! It is also not uncommon to read about a daughter who has been murdered by her own family for daring to befriend someone outside of their own race, tribe or religion. Why have the politicians turned a blind eye? Why do they let it continue? Multiculturalism? We seem to be more offended by words than by actions. As people, we like to feel comfortable in our community with language, habits and traditions that we all understand and enjoy. Strange habits and customs, if thrust upon us, can and do make us feel uncomfortable or alienated.

We, as a country, also act like a guilty prisoner in a court room of our own design. We feel guilt about the Commonwealth, guilty or ashamed about our royalty, guilty about the actions of previous generations; our politicians have even apologised for crimes and actions committed before they were born. Our Union Jack flag is frowned upon as being distasteful or upsetting to our foreign residents and guests, whilst in America the Stars and Stripes fly proudly on almost every home and business establishment in the USA. Throughout Europe, the EU flag flies happily alongside the flag of the local country, whilst British people frown if a couple of Union Jacks are seen flying in Great Britain. We British do not have a heritage that is virginal, but we have no more to feel guilty or ashamed about than the Spanish, French or Portuguese, the Turks, the Romans or the Greeks. We do, however, have things to be proud about. Our forefathers have spread education, commerce, transport, the

English language and wealth around the world, not to mention standing up and giving Hitler a good bashing to prevent Poland and the rest of Europe being taken over by this bully. Shhhhh. Don't let anyone hear you say it though, don't even think it!

How on earth did we beat Hitler and win the 2nd World War? If it all happened again today, we would undoubtedly fail miserably and probably criticise Hitler for the nasty words he spoke!

We have become like a nation of clumsy waiters, spilling the wine or dropping the dinner and apologising continually throughout the meal. Politicians do this on a regular basis; a thousand people needlessly and prematurely die in hospital through lack of care or medication. "I am really sorry. I didn't know it was going on. Lessons will be learnt." Maniacs, or should I say the mentally disturbed, are free to walk the streets unsupervised and unmedicated, to rant, murder and maim. "We are very sorry, we made a mistake." A member of the public is shot dead by the Police in a mistaken identity incident. "We are very sorry for the family and friends of the deceased," and a huge amount of money secretly changes hands. An off duty soldier gets murdered in broad daylight by an out of control religious extremist; "There will be an MI5 enquiry." The more money that these politicians and public servants get or have access to, the more they grovel and apologise for their ineptitude, mistakes and yes; wrong doing and crime. Of course you remember the expenses scandal? Inflated expenses were claimed over years by politicians and when found out, "I am very sorry, I made an accounting mistake," as if this relinquishes them of any responsibility and duties that they are paid so handsomely for. Their relatives are quietly placed in comfortable well paid jobs in government administration, or expenses are claimed for a second home that is being rented out, when it should be for the sole use of the MP in his or her own constituency duties.

I think that the public has had enough. Politicians, Police, the Courts, the Press and the general establishment are all viewed with suspicion and disdain.

We have all been taken for a meal in a dodgy restaurant with nothing but clumsy cooks, waiters and staff who apologise at every opportunity for their lack of skill, manners, judgement and professionalism. There will be no tip. We will not go there again, and we will tell all of our friends just how bad the place is.

The language of the people, a non-political language that resonates around the bars and the dinner tables of Great Britain, is clear; Enough of the political mumbo jumbo, smoke and mirrors, that the public have been force fed by the rich and out of touch career politicians for so long. Common sense and straight talking is the code that the public is now responding to. At the time of writing, we are leaving the EU, which so badly needs our money and so remotely tries to govern us. I welcome Great Britain governing itself again and making its own laws and decisions. A simple message, which carries a strong tidal meaning.

If I was an unwitting target, then the message struck home. In 1995, after going to a political meeting, it was suggested that I might like to stand as a representative for Waltham Abbey on the local Epping Council. I stood and was duly elected, beating the Conservatives into second place. My reasons for doing this were to assist in Britain leaving the EU and to encourage a more community based spirit in the local area. I was also only 100 votes short of winning the County Council election as well. I was shocked and surprised at the result, and I tried to learn the complexities of local government and understand just how local government works. In addition, I travelled on Eurostar to the European Parliament in Brussels with Nigel Farage, who took 80 of us newly elected councillors for a close look at just how the EU tries to rule Great Britain and tie the country up in 'red tape.'

On a more local note, I did my best to slow the tide of overpopulation and over-housing that is creeping relentlessly onwards, spoiling cities, rural towns and communities. In my five years as a Councillor, I tried to influence those with real power to get up and *do* something about National problems instead of forming more study groups, having investigations, apologising or sitting back and issuing sound bites for the press. Successive governments have failed in their duty to control the size of the population, and our present government is kicking the problem over to the Local District Councils with demands that they should build more and more houses in order to disguise the mistakes already made.

You may not agree with any of the comments in this rant, but that's just what they are, comments. We are the result of our environment, our upbringing, our education and our perception. Your views will be different from mine, but that is just the point; talk, listen and have an opinion. A different opinion does not make one right or one wrong. Everyone will see a single situation differently.

End of rant.

EPILOGUE

(Not really - I just want to keep on talking)

Somebody once said to me that I seem to have had two successful careers. I have certainly had the music and then the Karate as a way of making a living and having fun. Earlier on I also had the display work and the advertising, which I did find very enjoyable and challenging. If I had had the benefit of a good college or university education, I could have made even more success from this kind of work, studying graphics and design. I could also perhaps have gone into horticulture and been successful at that, in line with the modern trend of growing food organically and in an environmentally friendly manner. In today's age, I would have liked to go to University and study English, then perhaps I could have developed my writing skills as a testament to my great secondary school teacher, Mr Bailey. I have been happy doing most things, I have had a good life and have been lucky enough to have had relatively good health.

Looking back now, it's amazing how we can adapt and change. My metamorphosis came about between the ages of thirteen and fourteen. There were two basic life choices that I was faced with; remain a shy and introverted wimp, or have fun and enjoy everything there was to enjoy. I chose the latter, although this 'decision' was not really a conscious one. I faced these choices whilst at Tottenham Tech, with my lifelong friend Bimbo showing me an alternative direction in life to the lonely cell, which was my solemn guardian. Music was of course a great catalyst: Rock and Roll was going strong, Elvis was singing Jailhouse Rock, Eddie Cochran was singing Summertime Blues and Gene Vincent was singing Bebop-a-lula. It was a time of change for many, and music was our religion, the older generation looking on in dismay at the clothes, the music and the language of the youth that challenged everything that it stood for. We all can and do adapt, just as in nature, plant and animal life adapts and changes to suit its surroundings. I like to think I am changing, growing and adapting as each day, week and year throws up new challenges and changes. Indeed I have never thought of the human race being so very far away or different from the animal kingdom.

In her later years, my Mother used to say 'The worst thing in life is old age.' She hated getting old and hated looking at herself in a photograph or in the mirror. As the years unfold, I have also noticed the changes that age brings; bones creaking like the floorboards of an old house, a few tufts of grey hair here and there, then later on very dry skin on the forearms and wrinkles on the face. Eyes get smaller, or is it that the face gets bigger? The stomach gets larger as the belly button disappears inside (small) folds of blubber. Difficulty in reading the menu in a dark restaurant, and various other signs that old age is impatiently knocking at the door, remind you that you *do* have a sell by date.

Of particular surprise is my hair, slowly disappearing from the top of my head and making its way south to grow in tufts from my nose and ears. What on earth is *that* all about? I could understand it if, at twenty years of age, I had plenty of ear hair, as this may have provided my ear drums with some kind of protection from the thousands of decibels emitted by guitar amplifiers and PA speakers. But in my later years - what's the point, I'm half deaf now anyway!

At around the age of 15, most lads develop a small amount of upper lip hair which eventually grows into a moustache and requires shaving. In later years, the upper lip needs to be shaved every day in order to restrict growth and to enable one to eat dinner without a mouthful of upper lip hair being included in the meal. However, just lately, I have noticed in addition to upper lip hair, a lot of lower lip hair growing. If I don't shave for a couple of days the growth on my upper and lower lip gives me a walrus like appearance; quite scary really. You wonder just how Darwin would have explained the genetic benefits of these strange bodily occurrences and hirsute eruptions.

I don't however feel justified to complain about old age or anything else for that matter. One doesn't have to look far to see that there are many who are much less fortunate. There is and never will be, equality or fairness in the handing out of positive atributes. The clock starts ticking the minute we are born, and it jerks to a stop or slows down as and when it pleases. I am never going to look like Daniel Craig or sing like Tom Jones. I am never going to own a yacht or have the money that some politicians or footballers have. I will not say 'its not fair' - its life; moan all day, or get on with it!

I have not had to fight in a war (although if asked I would have), and compared to previous generations, I have had it pretty good. I feel guilty and humbly grateful when I think of all of the men and women of this country who have died or been injured fighting for our freedom from terrorism, invasion and destruction in other countries such as Iraq, Afghanistan, France, Germany and many other war zones and trouble spots around the world. This feeling is particularly poignant on Remembrance Sundays when we see that so many young men and women have given their lives for the freedom that I and we, enjoy so much. My mind returns to the time when the German bombers and rockets streaked across the English skies, killing and maiming so many with their packages of destruction, but sparing many of us 'war babies.'

I have been extremely lucky to have travelled peaceably to many countries with Lucy my wife, and again feel privileged to have done this, (my Mother never set foot outside of England). We have had some great times traveling to countries like Greece, Portugal, France, Belgium, Italy, Holland and further afield to Thailand, Las Vegas, The Maldives, Miami and Hawaii. God has been kind to me in giving so much enjoyment, although I am often considered 'jinxed' due to accidents that happen to me (usually near water) whilst on holiday. On one occasion, whilst in Mexico, I was lost at sea during a scuba diving trip. I pressed the wrong button and went shooting off in the wrong direction aided by the strong current, and subsequently lost sight of the instructor and the diving boat. I was rescued much later by a very worried crew after all of my survival at sea instincts had kicked in, as I surfaced and couldn't see ship or shore. This was *after* my very first scuba dive (remember, I have fear of water), when I was left alone sitting on the ocean floor while the scuba instructor took a panicking first timer back to the surface! The panic within me sitting alone on the ocean floor was very hard to control, but I knew that I would lose my life if I lost my nerve. I guess I was not meant to be a scuba diver!

I had always wanted to learn the art of wind surfing, and I got the chance on my 60th birthday in Thailand. Free wind surfing lessons were offered by the hotel, and after a preliminary introduction to the skill on the beach, I was in the sea with my board and sail. A wind picked up and I was thrown off of the board and into the sea, ripping one of my fingers on some very sharp coral underneath the waves. Blood was flowing, the doctor was called, and I was shuttled off to a hospital to have my little finger sewn back on. The date - 27th May - my birthday. There I was, eating my birthday meal with one hand, the other bandaged up and hurting.

On one of our very first holidays together in Portugal, I nearly demolished the apartment we were staying in and nearly killed both Lucy and I. I turned off the gas cooker after boiling water to make a late night cup of tea. We went to bed and woke in the early hours, coughing and spluttering. We felt drugged, and staggered out of the bedroom into the living area. The sun had started to rise and there was a noxious aroma that made it difficult to breath. The leaves and flowers of the houseplants had all dropped off, and it was at that point I heard the hiss of gas. Instead of turning the cooker off I had turned it full on, extinguishing the flame of the burner. We were later told that, had we flicked the light switch, the whole apartment may well have exploded, as it was full of gas! Luckily, we just turned off the cooker, opened the doors, and ran outside to get some oxygen.

This year, (2013), looks like being a much better year. There have been no real accidents or shocks whatsoever whilst on holiday in Kefalonia, Greece. Lucy broke a glass vase in our rented accommodation, but I have remained (surprisingly) accident free, apart from losing the keys to the villa and then having to travel to Argostoli to have a new set made. We have had a great two weeks of great food, sun and excitement.

I have had a lot of fun and If I am not being too greedy, I would wish for even further prayers to be answered. It is my sincere wish that there is reconciliation and friendship between all of my extended family members. I hope that my son, daughter and grandchildren find peace within themselves and contribute to the world that we all benefit from. If there is one thing I have learnt, it is that life is too short for petty bickering and squabbles, (although I am sure that I have done my own share in the past). It's a shame that we don't have the wisdom of old age when we are young; wouldn't the world be a better place? Or maybe it would be better the other way round, with young innocent children operating the brains of adults ruling the world.

I guess the world is not meant to be a perfect place, we are not meant to be perfect mortals, but just endeavour perfection, that is the test and maybe that is the secret or the reason we are all here on this journey.

I also hope that *Shotokan Karate England* continues to grow steadily and disseminate the knowledge, standards and ethics that have made it what it is today - honest and fair, different from many of the other larger Karate groups. Today, in 2020, we are in the middle of the Coronavirus pandemic, and so all of our clubs have had to close down until it is safe to reopen. I hope I have guided all of our instructors in the right way, to be firm and fair in their dealings with others, as and when things get back to normal and our clubs reopen.

It seems to me that every small action we take, and even every thought we consider, may have some bearing or some consequence, not only on our own life, but in the world we live in. It may be impossible to see those changes at the time, but when we look back, we can see the roadmap we have created by each of those seemingly subconscious, inconsequential actions. I was fascinated by a Peter Howitt film called 'Sliding Doors' where a character in the film has two distinct and separate lives, each life the result of small actions that were taken.

Of course, we also have the conscious actions that we perform; starting a new job, taking a trip or holiday, buying some new clothes or furniture, but I am talking about actions we make without really thinking about a plan or the future. It's as if when steering a small boat on a local river, the steering wheel can be unknowingly turned but no change of direction may be noticed. Further on, the change of direction may be noticed and an adjustment may have to be made. However, I do believe there is a way to guide that boat, or even guide your life; keep in your mind during every free moment the thought of your destination, your aim, or your ambition. Unplanned events do of course occur; sickness or illness, bereavement, war, or as we have now, the Coronavirus pandemic, but if that thought, ambition or aim is always kept there, in the back of your mind, you will reach your destination. Some may call this 'fate' or 'destiny,' but I think our lives may be a mixture of fate, our background thoughts and the small subconscious actions that we take daily. I have done this earlier in life with my music, Karate, and now with this book you are reading.

One thing that I often dream about is to speak to my Dad. A conversation with my real Father; just a day. Talking non-stop; his travels, his jobs, his photography, his work as a Remington typewriter mechanic, the war, nothing to hide. Just a day like this would make everything complete. Maybe one day...................

ENCORE

**'Do not fear failure, welcome it as
a step towards success'
Rod Butler**

W hen in the band and after a good gig,
we sometimes got requested for an 'en-
core.' The 'last' number of the show would be played and
the crowd would sometimes stamp and shout for more.
We would duly feign surprise and pop out onto the stage
again to provide the audience with a good rousing (and
loud) tune to remember us with as they went off home.
I see no good reason why a book can't have an encore,
and in the absence of rustling pages, banging front covers,
feet stamping and mouths shouting, I will assume that
I have an encore that cannot be ignored and come out
again onto the last pages of this book for a final number!

It seems ridiculous to me that each of us cannot leave this life without passing on some information
that we have learnt during life, to our friends, relatives
and the wider population of the planet. Geniuses such
as Einstein, Mozart, Darwin, Constable and many others,
naturally have done this, but there must be loads more
intelligence and knowledge unpublished, unseen and unheard of, that is lost forever. Just think of all the people
you have known that are no longer with us. So much in-

formation, so many interesting stories, so much is lost and gone. Much of what we learn and pass on during life *is* either forgotten or lost, or considered as the rantings of a decrepit and cantankerous old fogey, when we do eventually achieve old age. *Ask* your parents about their lives, how they lived, where they went to school, what jobs they had, and who their friends were. I wish I had done this. Many old people must have left these earthly shores with loads of valuable knowledge and information that has been lost forever. I think that is a terrible shame and always have an open ear to an older person who has had so much experience of life, and often (although not always), so much wisdom to offer. At the risk of benefitting from an enormous yawn or even a boo, instead of the cheers of an appreciative audience after a last encore, I will impart my pearl of wisdom to the foot stomping crowd of which you are an important (and I must add, integral) part.

I have been very impressed by the talent of a local young female singer; 'Adele'. As well as having a great voice, she has a wonderful natural rapport with her audiences, many of whom know her songs' every word. She is very natural, open and honest on stage, and during a recent TV showing of her Albert Hall concert, she explained that her next song - 'Someone Like You' was dedicated to an ex-boyfriend who finished the relationship with her to be with another. The experience of this break up traumatised her, but she thanked the ex-boyfriend for the painful experience he gave her in finishing the relationship. Because of the pain she felt, she wrote down her feelings. These emotional words became a song which she eventually recorded, and the song 'Someone Like You' became a very big hit record. The story may or may not be true but it is an excellent way to describe my own sentiment - *From something negative create something positive.*

Losing my own Mother in 1988 motivated me to break away from the Karate organisation that I was with at that time. Things in that organisation were not right, and I felt I could do better. It was a most difficult decision, with no guarantee that it *would* be a better situation for my own students or myself. My Mother was proud of my efforts, and the very small amount of Karate success that I had had. I felt as though I should make this change for her, and I always secretly thank her for that last little push or shove that she unknowingly gave me. The change proved to be positive, and the club that I ran went on to become more successful. More clubs opened and more success came my way. All of this success was a direct result of the change that had been initiated by the unfortunate loss of my Mother. Losing her gave me the strength to make some very difficult and far-reaching decisions - in fact, decisions that completely changed the direction that my life took.

If one reaches a stalemate or a blocked path in life, a negative event can be used to direct one's energy into making something better, changing direction, or making a long put off decision. Use a negative event or feeling as a catalyst to change, move on, or start something new. A negative event, however upsetting, can actually give you strength. I think this is even more applicable now in the midst of the Coronavirus pandemic of 2020, and when the disease is fully controlled we will hopefully see poetry, art and music spring forth, created during these upsetting and troubled times. As a case in point, this book would probably never have been com-

pleted without Coronavirus and the 'lockdown' that ensued.
 The show is now over, amplifiers are switched off. Ears are ringing. People are leaving, some looking dazed and bewildered, some excitedly talking. Torn programmes and plastic beer glasses litter the floor. The last night bus is about to leave. The drizzle is reflecting ghost-like images of non-existent passengers onto the windscreen. The engine is running and the driver is sitting, waiting patiently for the passengers to board. His eyes slowly close. He snores. Waiting.
 Applause?
 Yawn??
 Goodnight. I wish you well.

Life is a bit like a toilet roll - when you get near the end it goes very quickly! – Rod Stewart

The End

Keinosuke Enoeda - Tiger Of Shotokan Karate

The influence of Keinosuke Enoeda upon the World of Karate. A memoir written and published by Rod Butler in 2005 after many years training and assisting this great Master of Karate.

.

www.shotokan-karate-england.co.uk

https://www.facebook.com/WW2Facts

* * *

https://www.britishlegion.org.uk

* * *

Childline - www.childline.org.uk

* * *

Kidscape - www.kidscape.org.uk

* * *

NSPCC Helpline - 0808 800 5000

* * *

NAPAC Supporting recovery from childhood abuse - www.napac.org.uk

Printed in Great Britain
by Amazon